W9-AHF-788

From Idea to App

Creating iOS UI, Animations, and Gestures

Shawn Welch

From Idea to App:
Creating iOS UI, Animations, and Gestures
Shawn Welch

New Riders
1249 Eighth Street
Berkeley, CA 94710
510/524-2178
510/524-2221 (fax)

Find us on the Web at: www.newriders.com
To report errors, please send a note to errata@peachpit.com

New Riders is an imprint of Peachpit, a division of Pearson Education.

Copyright © 2011 by Shawn Welch

Project Editor: Michael J. Nolan
Development Editor: Margaret Anderson/Stellarvisions
Production Editor: Tracey Croom
Tech Editor: Scott Fisher
Copyeditor: Gretchen Dykstra
Proofreader: Jan Seymour
Indexer: Rebecca Plunkett
Cover Designer: Charlene Charles-Will
Interior Designer: Kathleen Cunningham
Compositor: Kim Scott, Bumpy Design

Notice of Rights
All rights reserved. No part of this book may be reproduced or transmitted in any form by any means, electronic, mechanical, photocopying, recording, or otherwise, without the prior written permission of the publisher. For information on getting permission for reprints and excerpts, contact permissions@peachpit.com.

Notice of Liability
The information in this book is distributed on an "As Is" basis without warranty. While every precaution has been taken in the preparation of the book, neither the author nor Peachpit shall have any liability to any person or entity with respect to any loss or damage caused or alleged to be caused directly or indirectly by the instructions contained in this book or by the computer software and hardware products described in it.

Trademarks
Apple, iPod, iTunes, iPhone, iPad, and Mac are trademarks of Apple, Inc., registered in the United States and other countries. Many of the designations used by manufacturers and sellers to distinguish their products are claimed as trademarks. Where those designations appear in this book, and Peachpit was aware of a trademark claim, the designations appear as requested by the owner of the trademark. All other product names and services identified throughout this book are used in editorial fashion only and for the benefit of such companies with no intention of infringement of the trademark. No such use, or the use of any trade name, is intended to convey endorsement or other affiliation with this book.

ISBN 13: 978-0-321-76555-0
ISBN 10:   0-321-76555-9

9 8 7 6 5 4 3 2 1

Printed and bound in the United States of America

Dedication

To my parents, Dave and Kelly Welch

For all you have sacrificed to my benefit, for all of the hours you have invested in my life, my success is your success.

Acknowledgements

Huge thanks to Dave Moser and Scott Kelby at Kelby Media Group for allowing me to perfect my craft and grow as an iOS developer with their team, and to Scott for taking the time to write the foreword for this book. I really appreciate the advice and support they've given me over the years.

Thanks to Matt Kloskowski, Dave Cross, RC Concepcion, Corey Barker, Paul Wilder, Erik Kuna, Tommy Maloney, and the rest of the fine folks at NAPP for providing valuable feedback on earlier versions of some of my apps. Thanks as well to Nancy Massé for always being helpful and for first introducing me to Dave Moser and Scott Kelby.

Thanks to Scott Cowlin, who first supported my crazy idea of writing a technical book targeted at designers, and to Michael Nolan, Margaret Anderson, Gretchen Dykstra, and the rest of the staff at Peachpit Press for helping me turn that idea into an incredible text. Thanks to Scott "Fish" Fisher, my tech editor, whose attention to detail in the code blocks caught even the smallest typo.

A very special thanks to Alan Cannistraro, Evan Doll, Stanford University, and Apple for teaching and encouraging me and other iOS developers, and for making their courses, lectures, and learning material available for free online.

Thanks to Cholick for being a daily sounding board for my half-baked notions and crazy ideas for nearly four years.

I'm grateful to my parents, Dave and Kelly Welch, as well as my brothers and their families—Eric and his wife, Gretchen; Danny and his wife, Katie; and Kyle—for keeping me humble and reminding me of the humor in life.

And, of course, thank you to everyone who uses my apps, my Twitter followers, my Facebook friends, and NAPP members across the globe. The success of an iOS designer/developer comes from experience; your feedback combined with your daily use of my apps gave me the experience I needed to write this book. Thank you.

—Shawn Welch

Foreword

Picture an iPhone in your mind. OK, now picture any other smartphone out there. Visualize this other smartphone until you have a really clear image of it. Got it? OK, good.

My guess is that whichever smartphone you pictured—regardless of the brand or manufacturer—it has a touchscreen, a built-in accelerometer, and rows of glassy-looking icons with a wallpaper photo behind them. I also bet that you flick the screen with your finger to move through your photos, right? Even though it's not an iPhone, it still works and even looks like an iPhone.

Apple did it so right when they introduced the original iPhone that nearly every new smartphone or tablet that comes out today is just another copy of what Apple has already done. But there's an excitement around the iPhone and iPad that no other smartphone or tablet manufacturer has been able to capture.

What sets iOS apart is the apps. Apps are it. They're "it." And while other smartphones and tablets now have some apps, too, they're not iOS apps, and neither the developers nor the end users of those other apps are rewarded like the people who design, and use, iOS apps.

The iPhone itself is a beautifully designed piece of technology. So is the iPad. Hold either of them in your hand and you can't help but like it. But it's the apps that make you fall in love. Everybody's iPhone or iPad has basic apps on it—Calendar, Maps, Weather, Calculator, and so on—but once you start adding third-party apps, it becomes *your* iPhone. *Your* iPad. It's personal because your apps reflect your life, your personality, and your passions. Apps have changed how we live our lives, how we run our businesses, and what we do in our free time. Imagine how powerful you would be if you could create apps that touch people, empower them, engage them, let them create and communicate in ways they never knew before.

Well, you're about to get that power.

Best of all, you'll learn how to unlock that power from one of the most talented, passionate, and gifted iOS programmers out there today. I know, because he's built numerous apps for my own company, and the number one comment we hear from everybody is, "Wow! Where did you find this guy!"

Shawn understands the end user in a way that few developers ever do on any platform. He uses apps the way we do, and looks at them from a user's perspective, so people feel at home using his apps. They're intuitive. They're fun. And, like Apple itself, Shawn knows that how an app looks matters.

In this book, Shawn gives you the tools to make your vision a reality, to design apps that people want to use and tell their friends about. He unlocks the secrets to what makes a great app and shows you exactly how to build them. Whether you're a designer who wants to bring your ideas to life, or a developer who wants to learn the power of great design, you're holding the one book that will open that door for you. All you have to do is turn the page.

I wish you the very best on this exciting new adventure, and I'm glad to see you've picked such a great guide to take you there. Now go design some really great stuff!

Scott Kelby
Author of *The iPhone Book*

Table of Contents

Introduction

CHAPTER 1

Getting Started with iOS

Everybody has an idea for an app. This is a warning from me to you, because when you finish this book and start telling people that you create apps for the iPhone or iPad, it will begin. Before you finish whatever point you're making, you will hear, "I have an idea for an app."

Naturally, as an app developer or designer, you've probably chosen to follow the unspoken rule: listen politely to these ideas and respond, "Interesting, that's a good idea!" Meanwhile, in your mind you're going over every reason why their app wouldn't work, how it already exists, how it has no potential customers except the person telling you about it, or why it would get rejected by the iTunes App Store.

So while everybody may have an idea for an app, we know that's not the end of the story or you wouldn't be reading this book. Few know how to take an idea, raw as it may be, design a rock-solid user experience for mobile devices, and ultimately develop that idea into a five-star app. Ideas are easy to come by, but the solid execution of an idea into an app is what iOS users have come to depend on.

On September 9, 2010, Apple posted its iTunes App Store review guidelines. To quote section 10 of these guidelines:

> *Apple and our customers place a high value on simple, refined, creative, well thought through interfaces. They take more work but are worth it. Apple sets a high bar. If your user interface is complex or less than very good it may be rejected.*

In other words, Apple considers user experience very important and anything that falls short in this area might be rejected.

Why Are We Here?

The question then becomes, how do you design and develop great apps for the iPhone and iPad? Before we can answer that question, it's important to understand what separates a great app from a not-so-great app: user experience.

User experience combines the user interface (UI), user workflows, animations, gestures, artwork, and overall *feeling* your app conveys to the user. Designing the best possible user experience requires an understanding of not only the user interface elements and navigation metaphors that are available to developers, but also the ways in which those elements and metaphors can be changed to fit the unique needs of your app. As stated by Apple in the iTunes App Store review guidelines, users of iOS apps have come to expect a rich and immersive experience.

You can't design an iOS app through simple screen mockups as you would a web page or even some desktop applications. iOS app users expect rich animations, gestures, and workflows. As a designer, you need to understand how to communicate not only a static screenshot, but also a complete user story to your developers. Often the only way to do that is by speaking the developer's language—or at least knowing what major factors are at play.

As a developer, you know that iOS is a powerful system that allows for deep customization of standard UI elements. Knowing how to customize an object to the unique flavors of your app will help your app stand out from the rest. Knowing what users have come to expect, and balancing knowledge with what boundaries can be pushed, will help you create the best possible user experience.

My goal for this book is twofold.

The first is to reach those who want to learn iOS app design. While code samples and technical conversations may stretch beyond your area of expertise, I want you to walk away from this book being able to look at an iOS app and describe the different UI elements, navigation styles, animations, and gestures in play. You should be able to sit in a meeting with a developer and communicate what needs to be done to transform the user experience you've designed into an app.

Second, for those who want to learn iOS development, this book is intended not as an introduction but as an enhancement of existing knowledge. I'm assuming some basic knowledge of how to program in Objective-C and or at least how object-oriented coding works in general. I want you to walk away from this book feeling comfortable with customizing and creating your own UI elements, animations, and gestures—the tools needed to incorporate good design and unique elements into your apps.

Of course, if anyone who reads this book walks away smiling, happy, or generally in a better mood than when he or she picked it up, that's always good too.

iOS Devices

One thing is certain: there will always be a new iPod. This has been true over the last decade, and I think it will remain true for years to come. No one can question the impact that the iPod has had on society. Interestingly though, in recent years the iPod has simply become a feature, or app, on an even more disruptive technology, iOS.

When the iPhone first launched in the summer of 2007, Apple released a new operating system (OS) called iPhone OS. iPhone OS was the most powerful operating system running on a phone at the time. In fact, it was based on the same core architecture used to power Apple's desktop and laptop computers, Mac OS X. What made iPhone OS special, however, was the addition of Cocoa Touch, a UI layer that allows the user to control the device using a Multi-Touch display and an accelerometer. No keyboard, no mouse. Point, click, and type were quickly replaced by swipe, tap, and shake.

Fast-forward to today. iPhone OS has only become more powerful. In the summer of 2010, with the launch of the fourth iteration of the platform, Apple changed the name from iPhone OS to iOS. The company's touch-based product line expanded to include not only the iPhone, but also the iPod touch and the iPad. This change also gave Apple the opportunity to bring functionality from iOS, such as fast-app switching and the Mac App store, into their more traditional desktop and laptop computers.

Table 1.1 outlines all iOS capable devices and the corresponding latest version of iOS they support as of December 2010.

TABLE 1.1 Apple Devices and Latest Supported Versions of iOS

Apple Device	iOS 3.1.x	iOS 3.2.x	iOS 4.1.x	iOS 4.2.x
Original iPhone	Yes	No	No	No
iPhone 3G	Yes	No	Yes*	Yes*
iPhone 3GS	Yes	No	Yes*	Yes*
iPhone 4	Yes	No	Yes	Yes
iPod touch 1st Gen	Yes*	No	No	No

Apple Device	iOS 3.1.x	iOS 3.2.x	iOS 4.1.x	iOS 4.2.x
iPod touch 2nd Gen	Yes	No	Yes*	Yes*
iPod touch 3rd Gen	Yes	No	Yes*	Yes*
iPod touch 4th Gen	Yes	No	Yes	Yes
iPad	No	Yes	No	Yes

*Indicates that iOS version is supported with some features missing like multitasking, background home screen images, and more.

iOS Development Tools and Resources

One of the nice things about designing and developing iOS apps is the quality and sheer number of tools and resources made available to you. Apple has done a very good job of building tools that are designed specifically for creating iOS apps. Further, Apple has built extensive documentation and reference materials on the iOS Software Development Kit (SDK) and the iOS Application Programming Interface (API). The four primary tools you will use to design and develop iOS apps are:

- Xcode
- Interface Builder
- iOS Simulator
- Instruments

Developer Note

To get started, go to **developer.apple.com** and register as an Apple developer in the iOS Dev Center. Registration is free. Under the free program you can download the latest version of Xcode and the iOS SDK, access a complete set of the iOS documentation, and run your apps in the iOS Simulator. By purchasing access to the iOS Developer Program ($99 per year), you'll be able to download prerelease versions of iOS software, install and test custom apps on your devices, and submit apps to the iTunes App Store. Additional pay structures for the iOS Developer Program exist for companies, enterprise programs, and students.

Xcode

Xcode is Apple's primary Integrated Development Environment (IDE). This application is designed for one purpose: to create apps that run on Apple devices. Development workflows for iOS are built directly into Xcode. You will use Xcode to write the code that becomes your app.

Xcode Application

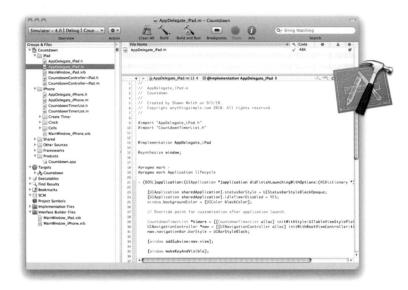

Interface Builder

Interface Builder is actually a component of Xcode and part of a suite of applications that makes development for Apple devices possible. In Xcode 3.1.x, Interface Builder is a separate application; however, with the introduction of Xcode 4.0, it has been built directly into Xcode's main application window. Interface Builder gives you a graphical user interface for creating UIs for iOS apps. You can drag and drop UI objects onto a canvas and create links between those UI components and code in Xcode.

Interface Builder Application

Designer Note

You can download Xcode and Interface Builder from Apple's developer website or at **fromideatoapp.com/download/xcode** (this book's website). While you need to register for the iOS Developer Program ($99) to submit apps to the iTunes App Store, you need only complete a free registration as an Apple Developer to download the iOS SDK, Xcode, and Interface Builder! Using Interface Builder, you can easily create and experiment with simple UI layouts for the iPhone, iPod touch, and iPad.

---

iOS Simulator

The iOS Simulator will install along with Xcode, however, you'll need to install an iOS SDK to run the simulator with apps created in Xcode. The iOS Simulator does exactly what it says: it lets you create and test iOS apps built using Xcode in a virtual iPhone or iPad environment, providing you with instant feedback and testing metrics. When you run apps in your iOS Simulator, however, the simulator will have access to the system resources of your desktop or laptop computer (processor, memory, video card, and so on). For this reason, the iOS Simulator is not a replacement for real device testing in terms of performance and related issues. Real-world devices do not have the power and resources of a desktop computer and it is essential that you test your apps on actual iOS hardware before submitting them to the iTunes App Store for review. Testing on real-world devices often reveals bugs in your program that were not evident in the simulator.

iOS Simulator
Application

Tip

The iOS Simulator application allows you to simulate the iPhone, iPad, and iPhone 4. You can switch between these modes by choosing Hardware > Device from the top bar menu.

Changing
Devices on the
iOS Simulator

Instruments

Every good app gets tested. Every great app gets performance tested. Instruments is a fantastic application designed for one thing: to give you real-time data about how your app is performing. Using Instruments, you can track in real time the amount of memory allocated by your app, the processor load, the frame rate, and more. One of the more complicated concepts for new iOS developers to grasp is that of memory management best practices. In iOS apps, the developer is responsible for creating and releasing variables from memory. When a developer fails to do so, the app will either crash or "leak" memory. Memory leaks cause screens to be jerky and negatively impact overall performance. Instruments helps you identify leaks, telling you when and where they happen in your code.

Instruments
Application

Quick Tips: iOS Development Strategies

Before we dive into the underlying technologies behind iOS UI, animations, and gestures, it's important to ensure that there is a foundation of knowledge we can fall back on. While it's not entirely necessary for designers to walk away from this book being able to write code, there are standard iOS development strategies that developers either must follow by design of the iOS SDK, or that they should follow as best practices. As a designer, knowing these factors that impact developers is crucial to understanding how to design the best possible user experience; as a developer, a quick refresh of best practices couldn't hurt.

Model-View-Controller

When it comes to coding principles, Model-View-Controller (MVC) is as basic as they come. At its core, MVC describes the relationship between an application's data, user interface, and "brain." By design, MVC keeps all three components separate. In the illustration below, you can see the basic relationships of the Model-View-Controller architecture. The darker lines indicate a direct association, while the lighter lines indicate an indirect association.

The Model-View-Controller Architecture

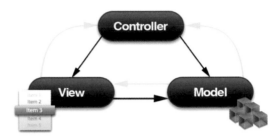

Model-View-Controller design is especially important with iOS apps. To help explain why, let's use the iPhone's Address Book app as an example.

Model

The model in MVC is where your app stores its data. In the case of the address book, this is all of your contacts. The model knows everything about every person in your address book, but has no way to present that data to the user.

Because the Address Book *Model* is separated from the *View* and *Controller*, as a developer you can access a user's address book contacts and repurpose the information in your own app. You can redesign how the contacts are presented to the user, or redesign how your app interacts with the data. Similarly, when designing your own apps, separating the Model from the View and Controller allows you to update, fix bugs, and repurpose code more quickly.

View

The View in MVC is typically the user interface: what users see, including the controls they need to use the app. In some cases the View can talk directly to the Model, but typically interactions with the View pass through the Controller, which decides what to do with that action.

In our Address Book example, the View would be the list of contacts you see on the device screen. When you select a contact in the View, the action is sent to the Controller. The Controller then pulls the necessary contact information from the Model and passes that information back to the View, where it is shown to the user.

Controller

The Controller is the brain of your app. Controllers typically dictate the app's navigation style and overall flow. While the Model stores data and the View presents data, the Controller determines *how* and *what* data to store or present.

Let's look at the Address Book example again, but this time let's search for a contact. When we tap on the search box located in the View and start searching, the View tells the Controller, "I'm looking for person XYZ." The Controller then takes that search query and decides how best to retrieve the information from the Model. Once the Controller pulls the necessary information from the Model, it passes it back to the View to present to the user.

Notice that the MVC architecture is very cyclical. Information and actions flow freely between components, but each component should be built so that these core tasks are separated.

Get the Code ➭ ➭ ➭

Download a sample app that demonstrates the Model-View-Controller architecture at **fromideatoapp.com/downloads/ch1#mvc** to try it yourself.

Subclass

Subclassing is another core principle of iOS development and a basic concept of object-oriented programming. Subclassing is based on inheritance, which means that subclasses inherit properties from the superclass or parent class. It sounds technical and confusing, but it's really not. Let's look at an example of subclassing that has nothing to do with programming.

Imagine you're buying a new car. You walk into a dealership and the first thing you see is a basic four-door sedan. The salesman tells you the car comes with a set of standard features and that it's available in red, blue, or silver. This car sounds like a good deal, but you tell the salesman that you really want the car in black and you want a built-in navigation system with satellite radio. Like any good salesman, he points you to the next car in the lineup, the SE package, which costs more but comes in black and has a built-in navigation system with satellite radio in addition to the baseline features.

In this example, you can think of the SE model car as a subclass of the standard model car.

When something is a subclass, it simply means that by default the subclass contains all of the properties and functionality of the parent class. However, the subclass can either override or add new properties and functionality on top of the superclass (without altering the functionality of the superclass). Or in our car analogy, the SE model by default has everything offered in the standard model. In addition to these features, however, you can override the car's color to black and add new properties like a built-in navigation system with satellite radio.

You'll find that iOS does the same thing with standard user interface elements and controllers used throughout the SDK. Oftentimes you can take advantage of these standard elements by subclassing them and customizing them to fit your unique needs. We'll talk about subclassing in more detail in Part II, The Basics of iOS User Interfaces.

Memory Management

As mentioned previously in our discussion of Instruments, a developer is responsible for creating and releasing variables in memory. This can be tricky for new developers, so what do we mean by "creating" and "releasing" variables? When you create a variable, your app allocates a small amount of memory to store the value of that variable. When you're finished with a variable, that memory space is set free and deallocated (to be used again in the future by a new variable). When a block of memory is not deallocated for a variable, it causes a memory leak, which simply means you have a variable taking up space in memory that is not being used or referenced by anything. When memory leaks pile up, your app becomes jerky and slow to respond. This is because active memory, a precious resource on mobile devices, is being wasted on variables that are no longer in use.

iOS apps are written in a programming language called Objective-C that uses the retain-and-release methodology for memory management. The idea is simple: every variable has a retain count that is affected by different uses of that variable. When the retain count of a variable reaches zero, iOS automatically removes it from memory when it is most efficient to do so.

So instead of trying to delete a variable from memory ourselves, we tell iOS when our code is finished with it by "releasing" it and decreasing the retain count. Take a look at the following code block:

```
1   UIViewController *myVariable = [[UIViewController alloc]
        initWithNibName:nil bundle:nil];
2   myVariable.title = @"My Application";
3   [self.navigationController
        pushViewController:myVariable animated:YES];
4   [myVariable release];
```

In line 1, we create a new variable in memory named myVariable. Immediately after creation, myVariable has a retain count of one. Line 2 sets a property in myVariable called title. Setting a title or manipulating other properties of the variable does not affect the retain count so at the end of line 2, myVariable still has a retain count of one. However, in line 3 we push the controller onto a navigation controller. When we push myVariable onto a navigation stack, that navigation stack wants to make sure the variable is around as long as it needs it, so it will increment the retain count.

After line 3, myVariable has a retain count of two. Because we don't need the variable anymore and want to turn over responsibility to the navigation controller (which increased the retain count), in line 4 we call release on myVariable, which decrements the retain count by one. At the end of line 4, myVariable has a retain count of one.

When the navigation controller no longer needs a reference to myVariable it will automatically call release on myVariable. Because myVariable has a retain count of one, when navigation controller calls a release it results in a retain count of zero and the variable is deallocated (removed) from memory. If we were to continue on with our code without calling a release in line 4, we would create a memory leak because the retain count of myVariable would never reach zero.

Additionally, had our code block called release twice, resulting in a retain count of zero while the navigation controller still had responsibility of the variable, the app would crash the next time the navigation controller tried to reference (the now absent) myVariable.

Note

Apple has extensive documentation and training tutorials on memory management in iOS apps. You can access this documentation at **fromideatoapp.com/reference#memory** or download it free through Apple's developer site.

Guiding Principles

When I started developing iPhone apps a few years ago, one of the first things I noticed was a lack of separation: for most apps, the designers were the developers. Of course, there were cases where teams were split for larger apps developed by corporations. But for the most part, designers were noticeably absent from the equation.

This struck me as odd. I know a lot of talented people who are capable of designing incredible apps, but they're hesitant to do so. I came to realize this hesitation was not because of lack of motivation, but rather a lack of knowledge about how to get started. Because of the closed nature of iOS development, unlike web applications, designers lacked an intimate knowledge of how iPhone apps are developed or the building blocks developers had at their disposal.

For iOS, Apple has put together a document call the Human Interface Guidelines. These guidelines outline some of the expected behaviors and best practices for iOS app design. Apple identifies the following core principles as crucial to designing and developing a five-star app:

- Aesthetic Integrity
- Consistency
- Direct Manipulation

- Feedback
- Metaphors
- User Control

Aesthetic Integrity

As both an experienced designer and a developer, aesthetic integrity is my personal favorite when it comes to iOS design principles. To quote Apple's Human Interface Guidelines:

> *Aesthetic integrity is not a measure of how beautiful an application is. It's a measure of how well the appearance of the app integrates with its function.*

Every app should have at least some custom artwork, but not at the expense of a positive user experience. For example, if your app is trying to present valuable information to the user, it's not a good idea to distract them with unnecessary artwork or animations. When it comes to creating a positive user experience, effective simplicity reaches more users than a flashy alternative.

Consistency

It's likely that yours won't be the first iOS app someone has ever used. Naturally, Apple encourages consistency between iOS apps and has defined a set of common styles and behaviors accordingly. Throughout this book, we'll address ways to leverage consistent behaviors to achieve the best possible user experience. In general, consistency in iOS apps allows a user to understand your user interface intuitively and immediately, based on their prior experience with other iOS apps.

Direct Manipulation

Direct manipulation implies that a user doesn't need interface buttons or controls to manipulate objects on the screen. Users can scale photos using a pinch-to-zoom gesture, or delete an email by swiping it from a list of other emails. iOS encourages designers and developers to consider objects or data as "things" that users can move, delete, edit, or manage.

Feedback

When users do something in iOS, they expect some form of feedback to indicate their action. The more obvious examples are spinners or progress bars that tell the user that iOS is working on something. Feedback is also important when indicating changes on the screen. Animation is commonly used to show users what changes were made. Consider the iPhone's Phone app: when a user toggles between the Recent and Missed calls lists, rather than abruptly changing the list, iOS animates the transition of the list, deleting or inserting rows as needed.

Metaphors

We'll talk about metaphors throughout this book, which makes sense considering we're creating apps to virtually manage data or perform a task. An English major would define a metaphor as a literary analogy between two ideas. Computer programmers use metaphors to draw analogies between virtual objects or tasks in a way that users understand. On a computer, files are organized into folders; photos are organized into albums. Some of the more common iOS metaphors include the card-style sliding navigation, switches for on/off preferences, and the spinning wheels of "pickers" to select from a range of choices.

User Control

Users expect to be in control of their apps. Your app should not perform a task or function without at least prompting the user first and giving them the option to cancel. If your app regularly checks for updates that are not vital to its function, it should allow users to disable this function. If your app schedules events, manipulates the user's contacts, or changes any local information on the device, it should not do so without first checking with the user. In the end, you should create apps that give users ultimate control—may God help us if an iOS app is the start of Skynet (iSkynet?).

CHAPTER 2

What Makes an iOS App?

Before you start designing or writing any code, it's important to understand what goes into an iOS app. This chapter gives you some background information on the iOS environment and the iOS app structure, including file types, executables, and resources. For those new to iOS development, you will find this chapter to be a useful reference with some of the more common files, resources, and settings mentioned throughout the iOS development life cycle and this book.

This chapter also provides some insight into the pros and cons of the iOS app runtime environment, that is, which resources your app can and can't access while running on an iOS device. In addition, we'll talk briefly about the primary configuration file used in iOS apps and some of the more common settings you will encounter. Finally, we conclude the chapter by going over the different types of iOS apps and the structure Apple has set up to categorize apps based on intended use. Remember, for those new to iOS development, our goal is for you to be able to communicate a designed user experience to a developer effectively. Learning what files go into an app will help lay that foundation.

iOS: The Big Picture

iOS is the operating system for the iPod touch, iPhone, and iPad. Apps for these devices can be downloaded only from the iTunes App Store. Chances are that if you're reading this book, you already knew that.

When iOS first came on the scene as iPhone OS in June 2007, Steve Jobs commented on its similarity to Mac OS X, the operating system of Apple desktop and laptop computers. Similarities in their core architecture still exists today and it is one of the reasons why iOS is such a powerful platform for mobile applications.

Similarities in the Core Architecture of Mac OS X and iOS

Applications in these two environments have key differences, however, that must be considered by both designers and developers.

Differences Between iOS and Mac OS X

Mobile apps are designed for short use, meaning that the user typically enters and exits an app quickly. Imagine you're a commuter on your way to the office. In the short time it takes you to get to work, you can pull out your iPhone, check email, start reading a book, and then switch to playing a game. This is not to say that iOS apps are designed for people with short attention spans—quite the contrary. Mobile apps should be rich and engaging to the user, but because the user can interact with only one iOS app at a time, it becomes increasingly important that he or she be able to enter and exit the app quickly.

Unlike desktop applications, mobile apps on iOS have limited access to system resources. An iOS app cannot interact with other apps on the device. This is often referred to as the Application Sandbox.

Application Sandbox

The Application Sandbox is a set of security measures ingrained in iOS to prevent malicious apps; these security measures block an app's direct access to files outside its own folder. Each app is installed in its own folder (the sandbox) and is only allowed to modify files and data within that folder. APIs exist for accessing system data outside this sandbox (such as Contacts or Calendar.)

When an app is installed, iOS creates the home folder for that app at */ApplicationRoot/ApplicationID*, where ApplicationRoot is the local apps folder on a device and the ApplicationID is unique to each app in the iTunes App Store.

Your app can only create or manage files that are within your app's home directory. Table 2.1 lists the folders contained in the app home directory.

TABLE 2.1 System-Created Folders in the iOS App Home Folder

Directory	Description
/AppName.app	The app bundle of your iOS app. This folder contains the actual files and resources you created in Xcode. *The contents of this folder cannot be modified.* Once an app is created in Xcode, it is signed with your developer credentials, distributed through iTunes, and can be installed on a device
/Documents*	Stores application data or user files. If your app requires you to edit and modify a file regularly, you should copy that file from your app bundle to the documents folder when the app first launches. Developers can also mark this directory as readable through iTunes, which gives you the ability to allow users to access files (such as audio or video recordings) created by your app
/Library*	Contains the subfolders /Library/Preferences and /Library/Caches, which store app data that are unrelated to the user
/tmp	Stores temporary files that are deleted between app launches. You can use the temp folder to story temporary or intermediary files before committing to long-term storage in the /Documents folder

*Developers can also create subdirectories within these folders.

When a user backs up an iOS device, iTunes will back up only the following folders in the app home directory. Any data stored outside these folders will be lost if the device is restored.

- /Documents
- /Library
- /Library/Preferences
- Any custom subdirectories created

Designer Note

Be aware of the impact an app has on user workflows. Because iOS apps are isolated from one another, your app cannot interact directly with another app installed on a device. If necessary, you can launch system apps, such as Safari, Maps, YouTube, and Phone; or your app can register a custom URL scheme that allows other apps to launch it. Besides providing initial launch parameters, however, apps can only launch another app; they cannot interact with its data.

Multitasking

Another big difference between iOS and Mac OS X is an app's ability to run processes in the background, called multitasking. Prior to iOS 4.0, when a user pressed the Home button on an iOS device, the app quit. In more recent versions of iOS, however, an app is not quit, but rather suspended in memory. By suspending the app and storing it in memory, iOS can quickly move from one app to the next, a process known as fast app switching.

Note

Multitasking is supported only on newer hardware such as the iPad, fourth-generation iPod touch, and iPhone 4. Devices that do not support multitasking will simply quit the app when the Home button is pressed.

When an app is suspended, all processes are stopped. This means, by default, if your app is performing an animation, playing audio, or downloading a file, everything is halted when the app is suspended.

In some cases, however, iOS allows certain special processes to be handed off when an app is suspended. These processes include

- Playing audio
- Location
- Voice-over IP
- Task completion (finish downloading or processing a large file)
- Location notifications (schedule notifications to display when your app is not running)

> **Developer Note**
>
> While not covered in this book directly, multitasking can be a powerful tool for creating rich iOS app experiences. You can visit **fromideatoapp.com/reference#multitasking** to find a few examples that explain how to incorporate multitasking in your apps. In general, however, it's important to remember that because iOS halts all of the processes of your app, you'll need to resume any animations or audio that were stopped when your app was suspended.

File Types

There are several common file types you'll come across when dealing with iOS apps. (See Table 2.2 for a list.) These files have varying roles in the iOS development life cycle.

TABLE 2.2 Common iOS File Types

File Type	Description
Header file (.h)	Declares the class properties and interface methods of their pairing Methods (.m) file
Methods file (.m)	Implements class methods or functions. Also called a Messages file
Interface Builder document (.xib)	An archived user interface layout designed using the graphical user interface (GUI) creation tool Interface Builder. Commonly called a nib file
iOS Libraries (.framework)	Provides access to various features in iOS. For example, to take advantage of geolocation services, a developer must include the CoreLocation.framework library in the project. Also called a framework

continues

TABLE 2.2
continued

File Type	Description
Property List file (.plist)	Stores a variety of data such as user preferences, app information, text, dictionaries, arrays, and even raw data from images or custom objects
App Bundle (.app)	This is your application. When you finish creating your app in Xcode and build your project, Xcode compiles all of the resources and files into an app bundle that is executable by iOS

App Resources

When you develop an iOS app, you will primarily be writing executable code in .m and .h files. In addition to the executable code, however, each app bundle has a separate subfolder known as the app resources. Resources are files provided to your app that are not executable code (images or audio, for example). As a designer, you'll primarily be creating assets that are bundled into the app's resources.

Video, Audio, and Image Resources

iOS supports a variety of video, audio, and image formats that can be bundled as app resources. To include an asset in your app, simply drag the resource from Finder and place it in the Resources folder in the left folder structure of Xcode.

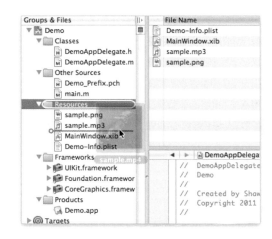

Some of the more commonly supported audio file types include MP3, AAC, and WAV; commonly supported video file types include H.264 compressed M4V, MP4, and MOV movies.

Tip

Visit **fromideatoapp.com/reference#supported-media** for a complete list of supported audio, video, and image types.

Nib Files

Interface Builder documents, or nib files, are also included in the app resources. As mentioned in Chapter 1, Getting Started with iOS, Interface Builder provides a graphical user interface (GUI) environment in which you can create your user interface. Essentially, Interface Builder allows you to drag and drop UI elements onto a canvas and save that UI as a nib (.xib) file, which can be loaded into iOS as an app resource.

Localization Files

When you launch an iOS app in the iTunes App Store, you have the option of worldwide distribution—one of the major benefits of the iTunes App Store. Because of worldwide distribution, however, it is often a good idea to localize the strings in your app. A string is a line of text, like a welcome message, or the description of a feature in your preferences. Every iOS device defines its local language settings. Localization files allow you to create a different set of strings for each language setting.

For example, if your app had a Settings button in the UI, using localization would ensure that the button text reads "Settings" when a user has English defined as their language, or セッティング when a user has Japanese defined.

Example of Japanese Localization

Info Property List

Every app has what is called the info property list (info.plist), which is created automatically by Xcode when you start a new project. This list defines global settings for your app, including app identifiers, hardware requirements, app icon file names, launch images, and launch conditions. You can modify these settings or add settings by selecting the file in Xcode. See Table 2.3 for a list of common settings controlled by the info property list.

TABLE 2.3 Common Settings Controlled by the Info.plist

Setting Name	Description
"Icon file" and "Icon files"	Identify which image assets in the app resources to use as the app icon. Using Icon Files, rather than just an icon file, lets you identify multiple icon files for each possible hardware configuration. We'll discuss this further in Chapter 7, Creating Custom Icons, Launch Images, and Buttons
Icon already includes gloss effect	iOS automatically adds the rounded corners and gloss effect characteristic of iOS app icons. This setting allows you to turn off the gloss effect as seen in system icons like Settings or Contacts (iOS will still add rounded corners)
Launch image (iPhone or iPad)	Defines which image asset in the app resources is displayed as a launch image. We'll discuss launch images further in Chapter 7, Creating Custom Icons, Launch Images, and Buttons
Initial interface orientation	Defines which interface orientation your app uses when launching. This can be useful if you're creating a game that has only a landscape orientation
Required background modes	Allows you to restrict your app to devices that support background processing such as the iPhone 4, iPad, and fourth-generation iPod touch
Required device capabilities	Allows you to restrict your app to devices that have specific hardware requirements, such as Wi-Fi, GPS, front-facing camera, video recording capabilities, and so on
URL types	Registers custom URL schemes that allow another app to launch yours

Application Types

When developing an iOS app, you do not have to define an application "type" by specifying it in your info property list or somewhere in the code. In the iOS Human Interface Guidelines, Apple groups apps into three categories according to their most common uses. Take into consideration that users are likely to spend more time in some types of apps and less time in others. As a designer, consider how people will use your app and which category it falls under.

Utility

Utility apps are more one-off apps designed for a specific use or function. Consider how the Weather and Stocks apps on an iPhone differ from the Mail and Contacts apps. Weather and Stocks allow you to jump immediately to a screen that gives you the information you're looking for, with settings to manipulate that view. These are examples of utility apps.

Utility App Type: Examples

Productivity or Navigation

Productivity or navigation apps are used to present a hierarchy of information or tools to the user. Characterized by the drill-down or sliding navigation, this is one of the more common app types. When you are designing a productivity or navigation app, it is very important that you define every screen and navigation workflow for the user. Keep in mind how users will flow from one piece of data to the next and consider not only the user interface of a given screen, but also how each user interface relates to the next.

Navigation App
Type: Examples

Full-Screen

Games or other immersive apps typically adopt a full-screen style. With full-screen apps, the status bar (which indicates the time, battery level, and so on) is hidden and the app takes up the entire screen. Users will usually spend more time in apps that provide an immersive experience.

Full-Screen App
Type: Examples

iOS App Blueprint

Introduction and "Hello, World!"

This is the first of five sections in this book called blueprints. Located at the end of each part, the blueprints will help you progressively build an iOS app using the concepts you learned in the preceding chapters. They are code heavy and assume that you have some knowledge of Objective-C and other programming basics. You can visit **fromideatoapp.com/downloads/blueprints** to download fully functioning project files.

Creating an Xcode Project

Start by downloading and installing the iOS SDK from Apple's developer site (see the iOS Development Tools and Resources section of Chapter 1, Getting Started with iOS). Then launch Xcode, installed by default at */Developer/Applications*.

When Xcode first launches, you should see a simple welcome screen. To begin a new project, choose *File > New Project* from the main menu, or click the Create New Xcode Project button in the welcome screen.

Choosing Your Xcode Project Type

Xcode provides multiple project types that make it easy to start building iOS apps. Each of these projects automatically generates a certain amount of code based on the type selected. The types to choose from are

- Navigation-based, similar to the iPhone Mail app
- OpenGL ES, typically used for 3D-style games
- Split View-based, available only for iPad apps and similar to the iPad Mail app, or the Settings app
- Tab Bar, like the iPod app for the iPhone, with black tabs at the bottom
- Utility, like the Weather Widget app for the iPhone
- View-based, a standard view-based app
- Window-based, a standard window-based app with very little code auto-generated

You can also select the product type: iPhone, iPad, or Universal. When you select Universal, Xcode generates the code necessary to create unique interfaces for both the iPhone and the iPad, but with one app file listed in the iTunes App Store.

Creating and Running Your First Xcode Project

For the purposes of this app, select a window-based project with the product type, Universal. After you select the project type, Xcode asks you where to save the project. Choose a location to save it to, and name the project HelloWorld.

After you save, Xcode creates the project and generates the code necessary to get you started. You can launch this application by clicking the Build and Run button in the main toolbar. This compiles the Xcode project and launches HelloWorld in the iPhone Simulator.

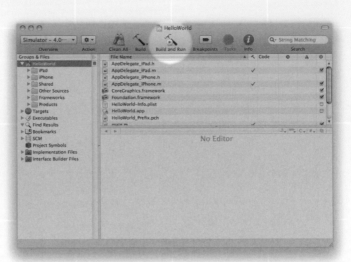

Making Changes to "Hello, World!"

Immediately after your app launches, iOS will call the function `application:didFinishLaunchingWithOptions:` in the AppDelegate.m file. We will use this function to start adding code.

Tip

Notice that Xcode generated separate folders in the left sidebar for iPad and iPhone, with AppDelegate.m files located in each folder. Because we chose a Universal app, iOS automatically calls the corresponding AppDelegate depending on the hardware on which the app is launched.

Let's begin by modifying the following lines of code, located in the *AppDelegate_iPhone.m* file.

```
1    #pragma mark -
2    #pragma mark Application lifecycle
3
4    - (BOOL)application:(UIApplication*)application
5      didFinishLaunchingWithOptions:(NSDictionary*)launchOptions {
6
7    // Override point for customization after application launch
8        [window makeKeyAndVisible];
9
10       return YES;
11   }
```

Because we created "Hello, World!" from the basic window-based project, Xcode didn't generate a lot of code for us. The big thing to note about the code that does exist is [window makeKeyAndVisible];. Located on line 8, this code tells iOS to make the main window visible. You should make any modifications before this line.

Add the following code to line 7 of *AppDelegate_iPhone.m*, immediately before [window makeKeyAndVisible];.

```
1  UIViewController *myViewController = [[UIViewController alloc]
                                              initWithNibName:nil
                                                       bundle:nil];
2  UILabel *myLabel = [[UILabel alloc] initWithFrame:CGRectZero];
3  myLabel.text = @"Hello, World!";
4  [myLabel sizeToFit];
5  [myViewController.view addSubview:myLabel];
6  [window addSubview:myViewController.view];
```

This code block does the following:

1. Creates a view controller that we can add to the main window. This will also be the main container of our text label
2. Creates a label with a height and width of 0, located at origin (0,0)
3. Changes the label text to "Hello, World!"
4. Automatically sizes the label's height and width to fit the text
5. Adds the label to the view controller's view
6. Adds the view controller's view to the main window

Your final code should look something like this:

```
1   #pragma mark -
2   #pragma mark Application lifecycle
3
4   - (BOOL)application:(UIApplication*)application
5       didFinishLaunchingWithOptions:(NSDictionary*)launchOptions {
6
7   // Override point for customization after application launch.
8       UIViewController *myViewController = [[UIViewController alloc]
                                                  initWithNibName:nil
                                                           bundle:nil];
9       UILabel *myLabel = [[UILabel alloc] initWithFrame:CGRectZero];
10      myLabel.text = @"Hello, World!";
11      [myLabel sizeToFit];
```

```
12        [myViewController.view addSubview:myLabel];
13        [window addSubview:myViewController.view];
14
15        [window makeKeyAndVisible];
16
17        return YES;
18 }
```

You should now be able to press Build and Run one more time. This time, however, you should see the text "Hello, World!" on the iPhone Simulator.

Conclusion

That's it! Congratulations; you've just created and built your first iOS app. In later chapters, we'll build on this code, adding new functionality as the book progresses. If you ever feel like you've gotten lost, just take a look back and make sure you haven't missed a step.

Get the Code ➡ ➡ ➡

Go to **fromideatoapp.com/downloads/blueprints** to download "Hello, World!" and all of the project files.

PART II

The Basics of iOS User Interfaces

CHAPTER 3

Physical Hardware

When designing or developing applications—especially applications created for mobile devices—one of the most important aspects to consider is user experience (UX). User experience doesn't just involve designing a user interface; it encompasses everything from workflows to input devices. User experience for iOS apps starts with the physical hardware.

The iOS platform is specifically designed for a mobile, touch-oriented user experience with minimal physical buttons or switches. Devices are typically held and can be oriented any which way. As a designer, you need to decide early on how physical hardware impacts the overall user experience. As a developer, you need to understand how changes to physical hardware can affect your app and how you can detect these changes to provide your users with the best experience possible.

Physical Input Devices

Physical controls that permit the user to interact with an application are called human interface devices (HIDs). These either receive input from or direct output to the user. By design, iOS hardware has a minimalist approach to HIDs.

Designers and developers should be aware of the iOS HIDs shown in the illustrations of the iPhone and iPad. Keep in mind that iOS hardware may contain some or all of these.

iPhone Human
Interface Devices

1   Power/Lock Button

2   Headphone Jack

3   Camera (Front and Back)

4   Speaker

5   Mute Switch

6   Volume Control

7   Multi-Touch Display

8   Accelerometer/Gyroscope (Internal)

9   Home Button

10 External Speaker/Microphone

Note

This list only includes the HIDs that most directly impact UI design and development. Additionally, each generation of hardware has a slightly different feature set and ultimately may or may not include all of the above controls. Visit **fromideatoapp.com/reference#iOSDevices** for a complete list of devices and features.

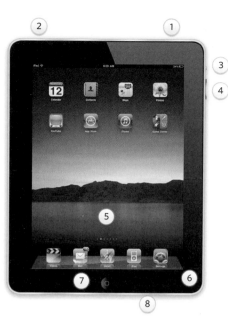

iPad Human
Interface Devices

(1)   Power/Lock Button

(2)   Headphone Jack

(3)   Mute Switch (iOS 4.2 and above)
         Orientation Lock (iOS 3.2)

(4)   Volume Control

(5)   Multi-Touch Display

(6)   Accelerometer/Gyroscope
         (Internal)

(7)   Home Button

(8)   External Speaker/Microphone

Multi-Touch Display

The Multi-Touch display is a staple of iOS devices. Capable of detecting
up to five simultaneous touches for smaller screens and eleven touches
for the iPad, the display is the user's primary means of input. Because
all of the app's input is handled with the Multi-Touch display, you are
not restricted to the same keyboard layout for every input, language,
or use case. For example, if your input field requires an email address,
you can select a keyboard layout optimized for email address input. We
will talk more about text input and keyboard layout in Chapter 6, User
Interface Buttons, Inputs, Indicators, and Controls.

Various keyboard
options in iOS

Audio Output and Input

From a user's point of view, audio output is pretty straightforward and behaves as you would expect. Your app can output sound through internal speakers at a volume set by the user. If your user has attached headphones, sound is instead output through the headphones. Audio input is handled either through an internal microphone or a microphone-enabled, one-eighth-inch headphone jack.

From the designer and developer's point of view, however, there's a catch. When including audio in your app, you are responsible for defining your audio's session properties. These properties include

- Audio session response to the hardware Mute switch
- Audio session response to screen lock
- Ability to continue playing on top of other system audio such as the iPod or other music players

Finally, your app's audio session will always be silenced during system events such as an incoming phone call. If you choose, you can set up your audio session to automatically resume at the end of the call.

Developer Note

Apple has made available extensive documentation including code examples and how-to guides for audio and video. You can download sample code and access the complete Multimedia Programming Guide on Apple's developer website or from **fromideatoapp.com/ reference#MPG** along with other reference material.

Camera

Recently, Apple started adding a camera to each device in its product line, including iOS devices. Currently, the iPhone 4 and fourth-generation iPod touch have both front-facing and rear-facing cameras while older iPhones have only a rear-facing camera. As a developer, you can choose which camera to access and how you want to use the data.

Note

If an iOS device only has one camera, that camera will be selected automatically when activating the video session. If an iOS device has multiple cameras, you can only access one camera at a time and must indicate which camera you would like to use. Finally, because the camera session also records audio, activating the camera automatically silences any audio sources.

Volume Controls

The volume controls on the side of an iOS device control the system volume. Your app and any sounds depend on this control. Through the iOS SDK, however, you can manipulate the system volume from your app. This means you can create custom volume controls within your UI to match the look and feel of your app. For example, if you are making a game for kids and want to match volume controls to your user interface, the iOS SDK allows you to control volume programmatically.

It is important, however, to be mindful of the external volume controls. Because the user can control the volume using the hardware input, your on-screen controls need to monitor external changes made to the volume and update accordingly.

Accelerometer and Gyroscope

Each iOS device is equipped with an accelerometer; newer models also include a three-axis gyroscope. As a software designer or developer, it is not mandatory that you know *how* these devices work. All you need to know is what these devices do and, more importantly, how you can use them to your advantage.

The accelerometer is a simple piece of hardware that detects the orientation and roll of the iOS device. When you turn your phone sideways, the accelerometer tells iOS that the device is in landscape orientation, and apps update accordingly. The gyroscope provides similar data, but instead of tracking orientation and roll, it tracks forward/backward, up/down, and left/right movement. To date, only the iPhone 4 and fourth-generation iPod touch have both an accelerometer and gyroscope.

We will discuss the accelerometer in more detail in Chapter 13, Creating Custom iOS Gestures.

Developer Note

iOS allows for different levels of control when using the accelerometer. You can access the raw data giving you fine control over orientation and roll. However, for most apps you can depend on built-in iOS methods. For example, when iOS detects that the device has rotated, it will automatically call the function shouldAutorotateTo-InterfaceOrientation in the parent view controller of your view hierarchy, passing as a parameter the new desired orientation. If your app returns a Boolean **YES** to this call, iOS will automatically rotate the main window to the new orientation. If you return **NO**, iOS will ignore the rotation.

Mute Switch

The Mute switch is used to silence iOS devices. Interestingly, the first-generation iPad launched with iOS 3.2 and a hardware switch that controlled an orientation lock (preventing the device from automatically rotating). With the release of iOS 4.2, Apple changed the function of this switch to a Mute toggle. When first generation iPads installed iOS 4.2, their Orientation Lock switch automatically changed to a Mute switch.

For iOS devices in the iPhone family, this switch also enables the vibrate function of the phone. This does not, however, automatically enable Vibrate mode for your app. If you want conditional sound versus vibrate based on the position of the Mute switch, you need to track and handle the logic within your app. Using the iOS SDK, you can determine the position of this switch, and it should be noted that any system sound requires that a device is not silenced.

Home Button

The Home button, located below the screen, closes an app and returns the user to the list of app icons. Starting with iOS 4.0, and supported on more recent iOS devices, pressing the Home button and closing an app does not actually quit your app. When a user presses the Home button on a background-processing capable device, the app's state is stored in active memory, allowing the user to jump back in where they left off using fast app switching.

An app stored in active memory is not the same thing as background processing on a desktop computer. When an app is closed and its state is stored, the app stops running. Any tasks, audio, or other processes your app was running are halted. Developers can pass off certain services such as large downloads, audio, and GPS location to iOS, allowing them to continue running, but these are not enabled by default.

Designer Note

Your app workflows should not depend on a user starting at a particular screen, but should be designed to allow a user to enter and exit the app at any time. Also, remember that iOS halts all processes and tasks as the app enters the background. This means that any animation loops or transitions of your UI are stopped and will not be running when your app resumes. It is the responsibility of the app to restart animations and remember their state when the app resumes.

Power/Lock Button

Locking an iOS device puts the screen to sleep without closing the app. Pressing the Power/Lock button has the same effect as not interacting with the device for an extended period of time. You can tell the app to disable the automatic idle timer by specifying that `[UIApplication sharedApplication].idleTimerDisabled = YES;` but make sure your app can wake up from sleep without issue.

When the device enters a sleep state, some processes continue, such as sound and network processes, but others are halted. Animations, timers, and other triggers stop and need to be restarted when the app resumes. If these processes are state oriented, you will need to save their state when a sleep event is triggered.

Device Orientation

When Steve Jobs demonstrated the first iPad, one of his selling points was that there was no "right way to hold it." The beauty of iOS devices is their versatility when it comes to orientation. If you rotate a device, apps adjust and optimize themselves to fit the screen.

As a designer, you should consider which orientations your app can run in. As a developer, you can programmatically determine which device orientations are supported by your app.

The iPhone, iPod touch, and iPad all support the following device orientations:

- Portrait (UIInterfaceOrientationPortrait)
- Landscape-Left (UIInterfaceOrientationLandscapeLeft)
- Landscape-Right (UIInterfaceOrientationLandscapeRight)
- Portrait-Upside-Down (UIInterfaceOrientationPortraitUpsideDown)

Determining Device Orientation

There are a few ways to determine the device orientation using the iOS SDK. The first is by accessing the device itself. UIDevice is a special class within the iOS SDK that allows you to access properties of the physical hardware. These properties include information like unique identifiers, system information, software versions, device (iPhone or iPad) type, battery level, and orientation. You can access the device orientation using the following code:

```
1  UIDevice *myDevice = [UIDevice currentDevice];
2  UIInterfaceOrientation orientation = myDevice.orientation;
```

In this example, the orientation variable would be set to the current orientation of your current device. While this method works in most conditions, it is not the most reliable when your device is flat, such as when resting on a table, or for apps that start in a horizontal position.

Another way to determine your orientation is to access the orientation stored in the parent view controller of your view hierarchy. (We'll talk in detail about view hierarchy and view controllers in Chapter 4, Basic User Interface Objects and Chapter 5, User Interface Controllers and Navigation, respectively.) Generally speaking, the parent view controller is what sits at the root of the main window. Each app has one window, and in that window you position a root view controller. The following code block demonstrates how to access the orientation of a view controller:

```
1   UIInterfaceOrientation orientation;
2   orientation = [myViewController interfaceOrientation];
```

Here, instead of accessing the device directly, we are accessing a view
controller that is within our view hierarchy.

Handling Automatic Rotation

One role of view controllers is determining whether or not a user
interface will support a given orientation. When a device rotates, iOS
automatically calls shouldAutorotateToInterfaceOrientation on
the parent view controller of the view hierarchy. When iOS calls this
method, it provides you with the new orientation and gives you the
opportunity to return whether or not that orientation is supported.
If you return a Boolean value YES, iOS automatically rotates the user
interface; if you return a Boolean value NO, iOS ignores the rotation.

```
1   - (BOOL)shouldAutorotateToInterfaceOrientation:
                            (UIInterfaceOrientation)orientation{
2       return YES;
3   }
```

Because there is little difference between UIInterfaceOrientationLeft
and UIInterfaceOrientationRight (or portrait and portrait-upside-
down), iOS provides the following convenience methods:

```
1   BOOL isLandscape = UIInterfaceOrientationIsLandscape(orientation);
2   BOOL isPortrait = UIInterfaceOrientationIsPortrait(orientation);
```

In line 1, isLandscape will be set to YES if orientation is either landscape-left or landscape-right; if the value of orientation is portrait or
portrait-upside-down, isLandscape will be set to NO. Line 2 demonstrates the same effect using isPortrait instead of isLandscape. If you
want your app to only support a landscape orientation instead of just
returning YES as we did before, you would return UIInterfaceOrient
ationIsLandscape(orientation). In this case, if the orientation is landscape, the resulting Boolean will be YES, otherwise this function would
return NO.

iOS Coordinate System

Prior to the launch of iPad and iPhone 4, iOS UI designers only had to concern themselves with one screen resolution. Because all iOS devices ran on the same basic hardware, designers knew that all apps would display on the original iPhone's 320 x 480 pixel display. This made the design process and asset preparation simple and straightforward.

With the introduction of iPad and the retina display featured in iPhone 4, iOS UI designers no longer have this luxury. Because apps can run on the standard iPhone display, the iPhone 4's retina display, or the iPad's 9.7-inch display, designers need to take additional steps to ensure UI consistency and image asset quality.

Points Versus Pixels with iPhone 4 and the Retina Display

Beginning with iOS 4.0, you must understand the difference between points and pixels. iOS uses a standard point coordinate system where (0,0) is defined as the top left corner of the screen. The x-axis extends in the positive direction to the right, and the y-axis extends in the positive direction towards the bottom.

As discussed above in the section Device Orientation, if your app supports multiple device orientations, iOS will redefine the origin (0,0) as the top left corner of the new orientation when it receives an orientation changed notification. New to the iPad and available to some iPhones starting with iOS 4.0, users have the ability to lock their device orientation. If a user has a certain device orientation locked, iOS does not signal an orientation changed notification and does not redefine the origin (0,0) as the top left corner of the new orientation

Before iOS 4.0, all devices were limited to a 320 x 480 display. In turn, iOS adopted a corresponding natural coordinate system of 320 x 480. However, with the introduction of iOS 4.0, *the coordinate system does not necessarily match the pixel resolution of the device.* As shown in Table 3.1, the iPhone 4 has exactly twice the pixel depth of the previous generation iPhones. This means the iPhone 4 uses two pixels for every point referenced in the coordinate system.

Device	Pixel Resolution	Coordinate System
iPhone 2G, 3G, 3GS, iPod	320 x 480	320 x 480
iPhone 4	640 x 960	320 x 480
iPad	1024 x 768	1024 x 768*

TABLE 3.1 iOS Device Display Resolutions and Coordinate Systems

*When the iPad runs iPhone apps in 1x or 2x mode, the iPad simulates a 320x480 coordinate system.

Fortunately for developers, most of Apple's APIs write to the device coordinate system by default. For example, if a button was set up to have a height and width of 100, and was drawn at the coordinate (10,10), this button would display with the exact same physical location and size on the iPhone 3G as it would on the higher-resolution display of the iPhone 4. Unfortunately, for designers, image assets need to be adjusted to accommodate for the varying hardware pixel resolutions.

Preparing Image Assets for Multiple Displays

The iPhone 4 uses two pixels for every point referenced in the coordinate system. This means that if you want to apply a background image to a button having a height and width of 100, the actual dimensions of the background image should be 200 x 200 pixels to avoid pixelation.

When designing an iOS app, you should provide both high-resolution and low-resolution files for each image asset. When iOS does not have both a high-resolution and a low-resolution image asset, it will attempt to scale the image to fit the device's coordinate system. The result is a pixelated image (when iOS scales an image up) or an aliased image (when iOS scales an image down). In addition to the risk of aliasing an image by scaling it down, loading an image that is twice the size needed for a display and then scaling it down when placed on the screen wastes precious system resources which are already scarce on older devices.

Naming Conventions for High- and Low-Resolution File Pairs

So how do you create a high-resolution and low-resolution file pair? As we will cover in Chapter 4, Basic User Interface Objects, an image object can be created using the following code:

```
1   UIImage *myImage = [UIImage imageNamed:@"mySampleImage"];
```

Without getting caught up in the code, notice that we create an image object with the parameter imageNamed:@"mySampleImage". This means that when the code is executed, iOS will look for an image asset named mySampleImage in the app resources. The good news is that with the introduction of iOS 4.0, Apple has made it much easier to accommodate various screen resolutions based on a simple naming convention (Table 3.2).

TABLE 3.2 iOS File Resource Pair Naming Convention

Device	Filename
iPhone 2G, 3G, 3GS, iPod touch	mySampleImage~iphone.png
iPhone 4 (high-resolution display)	mySampleImage@2x.png
iPad	mySampleImage~ipad.png

Using Table 3.2 as a guide, you can quickly see the pattern used when naming your files (Table 3.3).

TABLE 3.3 iOS File Naming Convention Pattern

File Type	Pattern
Low-resolution files	[your filename]~[device name (optional)].[file extension]
High-resolution files	[your filename]@2x~[device name (optional)].[file extension]

So when our code tells iOS to load the image mySampleImage, iOS first checks to see what hardware it is running on and then automatically chooses the file best suited based on the assets available. Similarly, we could have just created the files mySampleImage. png and mySampleImage@2x.png. Here, both the iPad and older generation iPhones would use the same image asset, but the iPhone 4 (designated as a high-resolution device) would load the @2x image file.

One final point: iOS can only automatically determine the appropriate file if all images are located in the same directory of your app's resource bundle. You do not need to define the path when referencing imageNamed in your code, but all images must be located at the same relative path.

CHAPTER 4

Basic User Interface Objects

This chapter has the potential to be the most valuable for designers wanting to start along the path of iOS app design. It is common practice for companies to develop websites with split teams of designers and developers. While it may not be obvious, one of the reasons teams can split this way is because the web designers *understand how websites work*. Designers are familiar with the tools at a web developer's disposal. They know how links work; they know they need to worry about hover state versus clicked state. They know how a drop-down menu and asynchronous page-load should function.

For iOS, however, this is not yet the case. To design apps for the iOS, is it essential to have a deeper understanding of how the user interface works than can be grasped by simply playing with your devices. The designer needs to know the tricks up a developer's sleeve and what can be accomplished in iOS. By the end of this chapter, you will have the same behind-the-scenes knowledge of key aspects of the iOS. We will outline the building blocks of iOS UI and walk through some of the fundamental frameworks used when creating iOS apps.

UIKit and Foundation

Remember that Cocoa Touch contains the UI layer of iOS. The architecture of Cocoa Touch can be broken into two primary base frameworks, UIKit and Foundation. UIKit is your one-stop shop for UI elements, hardware interface, and event handling. Because this book deals primarily with user experience, we will focus on UIKit. But you should at least be aware of the role Foundation plays in the iOS environment.

Foundation provides iOS a base layer of operation, defining NSObject (the root of all objects in iOS) and basic data types such as NSArray, NSDictionary, and NSStrings. The goals of Foundation, as defined by Apple's developer documentation, are to

- Provide a small set of basic utility classes
- Make software development easier by introducing consistent conventions for things such as deallocation
- Support Unicode strings, object persistence, and object distribution
- Provide a level of OS independence to enhance portability

Notice from our "Hello, World!" app in the Part I iOS App Blueprint that UIKit and Foundation were automatically included in the headers of our classes. This is because when we created our project, we chose New iOS App. Xcode knows these frameworks are required for iOS, so they are included by default.

Developer Note

The Foundation framework is an important part of the iOS development life cycle. If you are interested, I strongly encourage you to read up on the amount of control this framework gives you. All of your simple data structures, such as arrays and dictionaries (value-key paired arrays), are defined in Foundation. Additionally, Foundation defines utility functions for network operations and XML parsing. Finally, while Foundation and iOS are primarily Objective-C objects and classes, there exists a toll-free bridge to basic C representations of objects. This means you can move between the C and Objective-C representation of an object without any impact on performance. Visit **fromideatoapp.com/reference#foundation** for more information on the Foundation framework.

iOS Views

UIKit contains basic user interface objects. The basic unit used for displaying content on the screen in iOS is called a view. The parent object for almost all UI elements in iOS apps is called UIView. As mentioned in Chapter 1, Getting Started with iOS, one of the basic principles of iOS programming is subclassing. Because the parent class for all UI objects is a UIView, these UI objects inherit the basic properties found in a view. These properties include the size, location, opacity, and position in the view hierarchy.

UIView Object
Inheritance Tree

UIView

UIView defines a rectangle of a specific height, width, and location. This rectangle has basic properties such as opacity (visibility), background color, a record of its superview (parent), and an array containing a reference to any subviews (children) that may have been added.

In Chapter 3, Physical Hardware, we discussed the iOS coordinate system. The coordinate system of a view follows the same principle, and for good reason. When an app starts, it creates a UIWindow. Unlike desktop applications, each app in iOS is restricted to one window, and the entire app exists as subviews of that window. UIWindow is actually a subclass of UIView that has overridden the origin to be the top left corner of the screen and the size to the bounds of the device's screen.

View Hierarchy

When views are added to the screen, they exist in what is referred to as the view hierarchy. Much like <div> tags are used as containers in HTML documents, views can contain other view objects in the view hierarchy. This hierarchy defines the layout of views on the screen in relation to other views. If views overlap, the topmost view in the hierarchy displays over the underlying views.

View Hierarchy

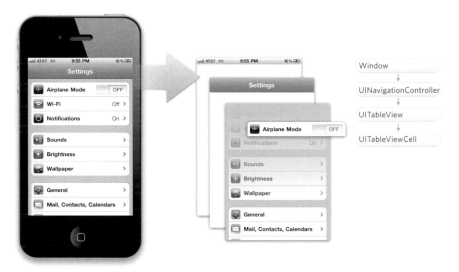

Managing the View Hierarchy

When a view is first created, it exists outside the view hierarchy. You can add a view to the screen by calling addSubview: or insertSubview: on a visible view. Additionally, you can build up your view hierarchy on a hidden view, and display after your hierarchy is complete.

Remember that iOS uses a retain-release strategy for managing memory. Removing a view from the view hierarchy decreases the retain count by one. If you intend to reuse your view after removing it from the hierarchy, retain the view before removing. Otherwise, it is possible for the view to reach a retain count of zero while you are working with it, resulting in an application crash. After you are finished using the view, remember to call release to avoid a memory leak.

Tip

For views that are reused often, such as UITableViewCells, you can use the reuseIdentifier tag. This tag lets you reuse a view that has been allocated to memory but is not visible on the screen.

drawRect vs. setNeedsDisplay

When a view is refreshed, the drawRect function for that view is called. This function draws content to the view every time it is called. Because drawRect is called often, it should be a very lightweight. Don't allocate memory in drawRect, and never call drawRect directly from your code. (We will discuss overriding drawRect further in Chapter 8, Creating Custom UIViews and UIViewControllers.)

So, if you can't call drawRect from your code, how do you refresh a view? The answer is to call the function `setNeedsDisplay`. Because resources are scarce on mobile devices, iOS attempts to optimize resource intensive processes whenever possible. Drawing content to the screen can require a lot of resources. Instead of manually calling drawRect to refresh a view, set the view as setNeedsDisplay. When a view has the setNeedsDisplay flag set, iOS automatically refreshes the view when it is most efficient. The time delay between drawRect and setNeedsDisplay is unnoticeable, on the order of milliseconds. But, by allowing iOS to call drawRect on its own schedule, iOS can optimize multiple drawRect calls and determine the most efficient way to execute the command.

Note

In order to optimize the performance of an iOS app, iOS renders only views visible on the screen. This means that if a view is off screen or covered by another view, iOS does not refresh the content in that portion of the view.

Frame vs. Bounds

Every view has two properties, frame and bounds. Both of these properties are from a simple data structure known as CGRect, which defines an origin (x,y), and a size (width, height). While similar, the frame and bounds of a view actually differ in their use and definition.

The frame of a view defines the height and width of the rectangle with the origin as the origin location in the view's superview. The bounds of a view also defines the height and width, but the origin is with respect to the current view and is usually (0,0).

Frame vs. Bounds

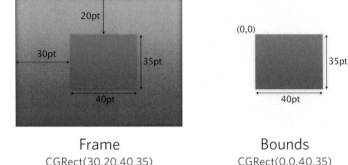

Frame
CGRect(30,20,40,35)

Bounds
CGRect(0,0,40,35)

UIView Example

Now that you have a basic understanding of how views work, let's look back at our "Hello, World!" app in the Part I iOS App Blueprint. In this example, we created a couple of view objects and then added them to our window.

```
1  UILabel *myLabel = [[UILabel alloc] initWithFrame:CGRectZero];
2  myLabel.text = @"Hello, World!";
3  [myLabel sizeToFit];
4  [myViewController.view addSubview:myLabel];
5  [window addSubview:myViewController.view];
```

In our first line of code, we create a UILabel called myLabel with the height and width of zero. UILabel is a subclass of UIView, so we know it has properties like height, width, opacity, and so on. In this example, we create a height and width of zero because we want to automatically size the view to fit the text, as seen in line 3. In line 2, we set the text of myLabel to "Hello, World!"

This is an important distinction between UIViews and their subclasses. A UIView does not have the text property. In this case, UILabel is a subclass of UIView, which gives UILabel things like height, width, opacity, and background color. But UILabel adds additional properties like text, font, and textAlignment.

Finally, in lines 4 and 5, we add our newly created views to the view hierarchy by adding them as subviews. In line 4, we add our label as a subview of the view of myViewController. After line 4, our label is not yet visible because only our window is visible on the screen. In line 5, we add the view for myViewController as a subview of our window. This adds myViewController and all of its subviews—including our UILabel—to the app window's view hierarchy.

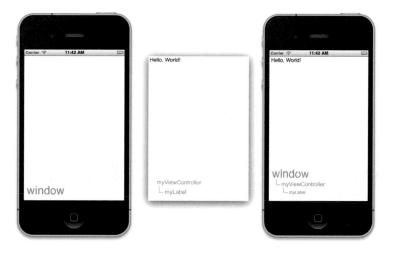

iPhone View
Hierarchy for
UIView Example

UIKit

UIKit contains all the objects necessary to build your UI. There are nearly a hundred separate classes defined in UIKit, so for the sake of brevity we'll focus on those objects most common to user interfaces. They include

- UILabel
- UIImage and UIImageView
- UIWebView

- UIScrollView
- UITableView and UITableViewCell
- UINavigationBar
- UITabBar

Note

In Chapter 6, User Interface Buttons, Inputs, Indicators, and Controls, we will continue our discussion of UIKit and cover the subclass UIControl. Go to **fromideatoapp.com/reference#uikit** for a complete list of the classes available in UIKit.

UILabel

You have already seen an example of UILabel in our "Hello, World!" app in the Part I iOS App Blueprint. A label is an interface object used to display text on the screen. The basic properties of a UILabel are outlined in Table 4.1.

TABLE 4.1 UILabel Properties and Descriptions

Property	Description
text	Static text displayed by the label
font	Font used to display the text of the label
textColor	Color of the text for the text label
textAlignment	Text alignment method used for the label. Options include UITextAlignmentLeft, UITextAlignmentRight, UITextAlignmentCenter
lineBreakMode	Line break method used for the label. Options include UILineBreakModeWordWrap, UILineBreakModeCharacterWrap, UILineBreakModeClip, UILineBreakModeHeadTruncation, UILineBreakModeTailTruncation, UILineBreakModeMiddleTruncation
numberOfLines	The maximum number of lines used to display the text. The default value for numberOfLines is one. Setting the numberOfLines to zero uses as many lines as necessary or possible within the bounds of the label
adjustsFontSizeToFitWidth	If set to YES, the label automatically scales the font size to fit the bounds of the label
minimumFontSize	If adjustsFontSizeToFitWidth is set to YES, this value is used for the lower limit when automatically adjusting the font size. If this limit is reached and the text label still does not fit, the content is truncated according to the lineBreakMode. If adjustsFontSizeToFitWidth is set to NO, this value is ignored

Property	Description
shadowColor	The color of the text shadow. By default, this color is set to nil
shadowOffset	The offset of the shadow for the text of the label. The shadow offset takes a CGSize structure that defines the (width, height) offset. The default offset is (0,-1) which means the shadow has a horizontal offset of zero and a vertical offset of -1. So, (0,-1) defines a one-pixel top shadow. Similarly, (0,1) would define a one-pixel bottom shadow

TABLE 4.1 UILabel Properties and Descriptions

UILabel Example

```
1  CGRect frame = CGRectMake(0, 200, 320, 40);
2  UILabel *example = [[UILabel alloc] initWithFrame:frame];
3  example.text = @"Hello, World!";
4  example.textColor = [UIColor whiteColor];
5  example.shadowOffset = CGSizeMake(0, -1);
6  example.shadowColor = [UIColor darkGrayColor];
7  example.textAlignment = UITextAlignmentCenter;
8  example.backgroundColor = [UIColor lightGrayColor];
```

Get the Code ⇒ ⇒ ⇒

Go to **fromideatoapp.com/downloads/example#uilabel** to download UILabelExample and all of the project files.

In this code sample, we set up a UILabel called example using a frame with a height of 40, a width of 320, and an origin of (0,200) in our super-view. We then set the label text to "Hello, World!" in line 3, and the text color to white in line 4. In lines 5 and 6 we set up a text drop shadow. For a one-pixel top shadow, we define horizontal offset of 0, and a vertical offset of −1. Finally in line 7 we center the text within the bounds of the label by setting the textAlignment to UITextAlignmentCenter. Because the label's width is the width of the iPhone screen, this centers the text on the screen.

Notice in line 8 that we set the background color of the label. Remember, because the UILabel is a subclass of UIView, the properties of the label are in addition to the properties that already exist in the UIView.

Tip

By default, a UILabel is opaque with a background color of white. This
means that every pixel in the label's rectangle must be filled. To put the
text on top of a background (e.g., text on a transparent background or
over an image), set example.opaque to NO; and example.background-
Color to [UIColor clearColor].

UIImage and UIImageView

Images can be powerful tools in iOS apps. The UIImage is a subclass of
NSObject, and part of the Foundation framework. A simple object, the
UIImage represents the data needed to display an image. The UIImage
counterpart in UIKit is the UIImageView. UIImageView is a subclass
of UIView, but it is designed for the purpose of drawing UIImages to
the screen.

A UIImage supports the following formats:

- Graphic Interchange Format (.gif)
- Joint Photographic Experts Group (.jpg, .jpeg)
- Portable Network Graphic (.png)
- Tagged Image File Format (.tiff, .tif)
- Windows Bitmap Format (.bmp, .BMPf)

- Windows Icon Format (.ico)
- Windows Cursor (.cur)
- XWindow Bitmap (.xbm)

Tip

To optimize your apps, consider using PNG files with a transparent background. iOS honors the transparency in PNGs, giving you the ability to adjust background colors with an image overlay while needing only one image asset.

When creating a UIImageView, you have the option of initializing the view with the standard view initialization method, initWithFrame. However, because of the unique nature of images, iOS gives you an additional initialization method, initWithImage. When you initialize a UIImageView with an image, it automatically sets the height and width of the UIImageView to the height and width of the UIImage.

```
1   UIImage *myImage = [UIImage imageNamed:@"sample.png"];
2   UIImageView *myImageView = [[UIImageView alloc] initWithImage:myImage];
3   [self.view addSubview:myImageView];
```

In line 1, we create a UIImage from our sample image, sample.png. This UIImage is not really an image that can be displayed to the user; it is actually just a data type used to store the image data, similar to a string, array, or dictionary. In line 2, we create a UIImageView, which is a subclass of UIView and is designed to display the UIImage data type. After initializing myImageView with our image, we then add myImageView to the view hierarchy in line 3.

UIWebView

The UIWebView object is used to embed web-based content. You can choose to load a network request and pull content from the Internet, or you can use local resources from your app bundle and load an HTML formatted string. The UIWebView can also be used to display additional file types such as Excel (.xls), Keynote (.key.zip), Numbers (.numbers.zip), Pages (.pages.zip), PDF (.pdf), PowerPoint (.ppt), Rich Text Format (.rtf), and Word (.doc).

TABLE 4.2
Properties,
Methods, and
Descriptions

Property and Method	Description
`delegate`	The delegate is sent messages while the content is loading or when actions, such as selecting a link, are taken within the UIWebView
`request`	This parameter represents the NSURLRequest object of the web view's loaded, or currently loading content. This value can only be set with the loadRequest: method
`loading`	Defined as a Boolean, YES or NO, this value indicates whether or not the UIWebView is finished loading the request
`canGoBack`	A Boolean value that defines whether or not the UIWebView can navigate backward. If YES, you must still implement a Back button that calls the method goBack:
`canGoForward`	A Boolean value that defines whether or not the UIWebView can navigate forward. If YES, you must still implement a Forward button that calls the method goForward:
`dataDetectorTypes`	Defines the behavior of the UIWebView when auto-detecting data types. Options include UIDataDetectorTypePhoneNumber, UIDataDetectorTypeLink, UIDataDetectorTypeAddress, UIDataDetectorTypeCalendarEvent, UIDataDetectorTypeNone, and UIDataDetectorTypeAll. If a data type detector is defined, iOS automatically converts detected data patterns into links that activate corresponding iOS functions. For example, phone numbers turn into links that, when tapped, prompt the user to initiate a phone call

UIWebView Example

Here we show a simple web browser implemented using UIWebView. The following code block creates a loading label and adds it to our window. You'll notice that we set hidden to YES on our loading label. This means that even though the label is in the view hierarchy, it will not be visible.

```
1    CGRect frame = CGRectMake(0, 200, 320, 40);
2    myLoadingLabel = [[UILabel alloc] initWithFrame:frame];
3    myLoadingLabel.text = @"Loading...";
4    myLoadingLabel.textAlignment = UITextAlignmentCenter;
5    myLoadingLabel.hidden = YES;
6    [window addSubview:myLoadingLabel];
7
8    frame = CGRectMake(0, 20, 320, 460);
```

```
9   myWebView = [[UIWebView alloc] initWithFrame:frame];

10

11  NSURL *homeURL = [NSURL URLWithString:@"http://fromideatoapp.com"];
12  NSURLRequest *request = [[NSURLRequest alloc] initWithURL:homeURL];

13

14  myWebView setDelegate:self];
15  [myWebView loadRequest:request];
16  [request release];
```

Get the Code ⇒⇒⇒

Go to **fromideatoapp.com/downloads/example#uiwebview** to download
UIWebView and all of the project files.

Most of this code block should look familiar from our previous experience with UILabel. Lines 11 and 12 are used to create our request
object. First we create an NSURL, then we allocate a new request variable using that URL. Once we have a request ready, all we need to do
is apply it to our UIWebView, myWebView.

Before we can do that, however, we have to set up our UIWebView delegate. Here we are just setting it to self, which means myWebView will
look to the current class to implement any delegate methods. In this
case, we care about webViewDidStartLoad and webViewDidFinish-
Load. These delegate methods are implemented in the next code block.

>_   **Developer Note**

Delegates are important in iOS programming. The delegate is
called when an object is ready to perform specific functions. For
example, UIWebView defines the protocol UIWebViewDelegate.
In this delegate protocol, you will find optional methods such as
`webViewDidStartLoad:(UIWebView *)webView`. When the UIWeb-
View starts loading its request, it will call `webViewDidStartLoad` in
its assigned delegate method. This gives you the control to perform
the necessary action. If you are unfamiliar with the delegate programming practice, I strongly suggest Apple's developer documentation at **fromideatoapp.com/reference#delegates** for further reading.

```
1    - (void)webViewDidStartLoad:(UIWebView *)webView{
2        myLoadingLabel.hidden = NO;
3        UIApplication *application = [UIApplication sharedApplication];
4        application.networkActivityIndicatorVisible = YES;
5    }
6
7    - (void)webViewDidFinishLoad:(UIWebView *)webView{
8        myLoadingLabel.hidden = YES;
9        UIApplication *application = [UIApplication sharedApplication];
10       application.networkActivityIndicatorVisible = NO;
11       [window addSubview:webView];
12   }
```

Lines 1 through 4 in this code block implement `webViewDidStartLoad`. When a UIWebView begins loading its request, it calls this method on its delegate. We'll take advantage of this call by first making our loading label visible and turning on the device network activity indicator. Lines 6 through 10 implement `webViewDidFinishLoad`. Here, our UIWebView has finished loading its request and we want to add it to our window. In line 7 we hide the loading label, and in line 8 we hide the device network activity indicator. Finally, now that our UIWebView has finished loading the request, we add it as a subview to the main window.

Designer Note

It is common for iOS apps to use loading screens. As you design apps, consider the type and amount of data your screens are loading. If you need to load data from the Internet, or from large data sets, design loading screens to handle the asynchronous operations. There are default UIViews in iOS to indicate progress, including progress bars and activity spinners. Additionally, if your views require that content be loaded from the Internet, design screens to handle conditions where there is no Internet connection available.

UIScrollView

A UIScrollView is a special class used for displaying content that is larger than the bounds of the screen. If scrolling is enabled, this class automatically handles pinch-to-zoom and pan gestures using delegate methods to control content. Table 4.3 highlights some of the more unique properties of UIScrollView that we'll cover in this chapter. If you go to **fromideatoapp.com/reference#uiscrollview** you can find a complete list of the properties from Apple's developer documentation.

Note

Avoid embedding UIScrollViews, UITableViews, and UIWebViews as subviews of each other. Because iOS automatically handles the touch events controlling scroll or pinch-to-zoom gestures, embedding a scroll view within another scroll view can result in unexpected behavior as the receiver of the touch event could be improperly handled or unknown.

Property	Description
`delegate`	The delegate called when UIScrollView encounters specific events
`contentOffset`	Defined as a CGPoint (x,y), this value is the offset of the origin of the contentView inside the UIScrollView
`contentSize`	The size of the contentView within the UIScrollView. The contentView is typically larger than the bounds of the UIScrollView, which allows the user to scroll and reveal hidden content
`scrollEnabled`	A Boolean value that enables or disables scrolling within the UIScrollView
`directionalLockEnabled`	Diagonal scrolling is permitted only when directionalLockEnabled is set to NO, which is the default value. When directional lock is enabled, at any given time a user is only able to scroll either vertically or horizontally, but not both at the same time. A user who starts scrolling vertically will be locked into a vertical scroll until dragging ends; the same would apply to horizontal scrolling
`scrollsToTop`	If scrollsToTop is set to YES, iOS automatically scrolls the UIScrollView to a contentOffset y value of 0 when the user double taps the iOS status bar. iOS will not scroll the x component of contentOffset

TABLE 4.3
UIScrollView Properties and Descriptions

continues

TABLE 4.3
continued

Property	Description
pagingEnabled	If pagingEnabled is set to YES, the UIScrollView will settle on contentOffset values that are multiples of the bounds of UIScrollView. The best example of this is actually the iPhone app launcher screen. All of the app icons exist in the same UIScrollView. When you swipe left or right, the UIScrollView settles on the nearest contentOffset that is a multiple of the width of the screen—this creates the pages
indicatorStyle	The bar style of the UIScrollView indicators. Options include UIScrollViewIndicatorStyleDefault, UIScrollViewIndicatorStyleBlack, and UIScrollViewIndicatorWhite

UIScrollView Example

The following example demonstrates a simple UIScrollView with paging enabled. You'll notice that the behavior is similar to that of the iOS app launch screen. Lines 1 and 2 simply set up some constants used to create our scroll view demo. In line 4, we initialize a scrollView using our frame. Notice we set the bounds of the scrollView to a width of 320, or the width of an iPhone or iPod touch screen. In line 5, we set up our scrollView's contentSize. For this example we want the contentSize, or the scrollable area, of the UIScrollView to be the width of the screen times the number of pages. Finally, we set pagingEnabled = YES, which tells the scrollView to settle on contentOffsets that are multiples of the bounds of our scrollView, or multiples of 320 along the horizontal axis.

Lines 8 through 27 look a little complicated, but let me break down what we're doing. For each page of the scroll view, we want to create a UIView and add it as a subview to scrollView. To do this, the first thing we did was set up a for-loop to iterate through the number of pages defined in line 2. Because the origin of each "page" needs to be offset in the superview, we created a new frame with the x value 320 times our iteration variable. For page 0, this will evaluate to 0; for page 1, this will evaluate to 320. This pattern will continue through each page. Lines 11 through 21 simply create a UIView, set the background to an alternating white or light gray color, and then create a centered UILabel indicating the page number. Finally at the end of our loop, we add our view to scrollView and take care of some memory management.

```
1    CGRect frame = CGRectMake(0, 0, 320, 480);
2    int pageCount = 6;
3
4    UIScrollView *scrollView = [[UIScrollView alloc] initWithFrame:frame];
5    scrollView.contentSize = CGSizeMake(320*pageCount, 480);
6    scrollView.pagingEnabled = YES;
7
8    for (int i=0; i<pageCount; i++) {
9        CGRect f = CGRectMake(i*320, 0, 320, 480);
10       UIView *v = [[UIView alloc] initWithFrame:f];
11       if(i%2)
12         v.backgroundColor = [UIColor whiteColor];
13       else
14         v.backgroundColor = [UIColor lightGrayColor];
15
16       UILabel *l = [[UILabel alloc] initWithFrame:v.bounds];
17       l.text = [NSString stringWithFormat:@"View #%d",i+1];
18       l.backgroundColor = [UIColor clearColor];
19       l.textAlignment = UITextAlignmentCenter;
20       [v addSubview:l];
21       [scrollView addSubview:v];
22
23       [v release];
24       [l release];
25   }
26
27   [window addSubview:scrollView];
```

Get the Code ⇒ ⇒ ⇒

Download UIScrollView and all of the project files at **fromideatoapp.com/downloads/example#uiscrollview**. Try experimenting with some of the UIScrollView properties mentioned in this chapter.

UITableView and UITableViewCell

UITableViews are among the most common UI objects used in iOS. UITableViews display content in the Mail app, SMS Chat, Settings, Safari History, and more. For the most part, any time you encounter content that scrolls vertically, it is accomplished with a UITableView. UITableView is a subclass of UIScrollView, but instead of defining the contentSize of the scrollView directly, you define the number of sections and rows within the UITableView and their heights, respectively. iOS automatically determines the appropriate size of the scrollView content.

With UITableViews come UITableViewCells. A UITableViewCell is a single row within the UITableView. Picture the iPhone's default mail app. The UITableView represents the entire scrollView used to scroll through your mail messages. A UITableViewCell is used to represent each individual message.

UITableView and
UITableViewCell

Each UITableViewCell is a subview of the UITableView. However, instead of allocating a new UITableViewCell to represent each cell in memory, iOS will reuse cells so only a small number are allocated at a time. When a cell scrolls off the screen, it becomes available for reuse. As the screen scrolls a new cell into view, it retrieves cells that are available for reuse and repositions them in the superview. This means a table containing 100,000 cells would allocate as much memory to and have equal performance as a table containing only ten cells.

Because UITableViews are so common in iOS user interfaces, we will dedicate the entirety of Chapter 9, Creating Custom Table Views, to this topic.

UIToolbar

The UIToolbar is a common UI element used to present users with a set of options. UIToolbars are typically positioned at the bottom of the screen on iPhone apps, but they can be positioned almost anywhere in iPad workflows. The most common example of a UIToolbar is found in the Safari application.

Safari Toolbar

UIToolbar

In Safari for the iPhone, the blue toolbar at the bottom is a UIToolbar containing quick access to frequent actions such as navigate back, navigate forward, bookmark, history, and open pages. You will notice that when the iPhone rotates to portrait orientation, the toolbar icon automatically redistributes to fill the width of the UIToolbar.

Property	Description
barStyle	iOS provides some default barStyle values for commonly used settings. Options include UIBarStyleDefault, UIBarStyleBlack, UIBarStyleBlackOpaque, and UIBarStyleTranslucent
tintColor	Setting the tintColor of UIToolbar colorizes the UIToolbar with any given color
translucent	A Boolean value that defines whether or not the UIToolbar is translucent
items	An array of UIBarButtonItems used to display in the UIToolbar. You can either choose from one of many system items or create your own custom UIBarButtonItem

TABLE 4.4 UIToolbar Properties and Descriptions

Developer Note

The items in a UIToolbar float from left to right. So, if you have two buttons in the items array, they will be floated left in the UIToolbar as far as possible. If you want to separate UIBarButtons-Item items with space (e.g., creating left and right button items), separate them in the items array using the system UIBarButtonItem, UIBarButtonSystemItemFlexibleSpace. This will place flexible space between the remaining two buttons pushing them to the left and right edges.

CHAPTER 5

User Interface Controllers and Navigation

So far we've learned that there are a variety of UI objects and that all of these objects are descendants of the same UIView superclass. This UIView superclass operates as a foundation, or canvas, for most UI elements in iOS by defining a rectangle of specific size and location in which UI elements can be drawn. We've learned that these views can be added to one another to build up a view hierarchy. In a nutshell, you should have a good grasp of what actually defines an element in iOS user interface and what building blocks and frameworks are at your disposal. What we haven't discussed is how to manage those views or view hierarchy in iOS.

Remember one of the core iOS development strategies is Model-View-Controller (MVC). Applications designed around MVC separate the application's data models, user interfaces, and logic centers. Appropriately, UIViews typically represent the view portion of MVC; the next step is to learn about controllers.

What Is a Controller?

Simply put, a controller is the logic center of your app. A controller takes a piece of information from one source and then decides what the next action should be. This information could be provided through user input or through events called by the iOS runtime environment itself. In this way, controllers are used to manage the behavior of views or a collection of views in iOS apps.

iOS has a subset of controller classes specifically designed to manage different use-case scenarios and navigation styles. The root of all of these classes is called the UIViewController. The UIViewController class sets up a UIView and defines an interface for interacting with this view or responding to other system events that may occur.

We have already seen an example of a UIViewController. Here is a code block that may look familiar from Chapter 3, Physical Hardware, where we discussed how to handle automatic device rotation.

```
1   - (BOOL)shouldAutorotateToInterfaceOrientation:
                        (UIInterfaceOrientation)orientation{
2       return YES;
3   }
```

This function, shouldAutorotateToInterfaceOrientation, is defined in the interface of the UIViewController class. When a UIViewController is loaded into memory, iOS automatically calls this function asking whether or not it is OK to rotate the interface of that view controller to a new interface orientation. If your UIViewController returns YES, iOS rotates the screen and redefines the origin (0,0) to the top-left corner of the new orientation. Remember, our model-view-controller relationship keeps all of the decisions centered in the controller. By defining should-AutoRotateToInterfaceOrientation in the UIViewController class, iOS makes it the responsibility of our controller to decide whether or not it is OK to rotate.

Note

If you have multiple UIViewControllers loaded on the screen, they must all be in agreement on the behavior of shouldAutorotateToInterface-Orientation. To rotate, all view controllers must return YES—if one UIViewController returns NO, the screen will not rotate.

Much the same way all UI objects stem from a UIView, all native controller classes stem from UIViewController. In this chapter, we'll cover the following UIViewController subclasses:

- UITabBarController
- UINavigationController
- UISplitViewController

We'll also take a look at the UIPopoverController, which is an iPad-specific container object for displaying a UIViewController as a layer on top of another UIViewController. Finally, we'll look at the special modal view relationship UIViewControllers can share.

Before we get into detail on the navigation-based view controllers, however, let's take a step back and talk about our base class, the UIViewController. Remember that the native view controller subclasses are extensions of the parent class. This means that all of the functions discussed in the UIViewController class are also available in these subclasses.

Designer Note

Don't feel limited or restricted to design apps that fit exactly with the native UIViewController subclasses. The native subclasses are an excellent starting place for custom UI and you are free to build on them to make them your own. Keep in mind, however, that Apple is very strict when it comes to human interface guidelines. You are more than welcome to change or add custom features to your controllers or navigation styles, but you must do so within the guidelines presented. These guidelines include standards for button size, location, navigation expectations, and so on. A complete list of these guidelines is available for free at **fromideatoapp.com/reference#hig** along with samples and other reference material.

UIViewController

UIViewControllers manage the life cycle of a UIView. This includes the creation, duration, and destruction of a UIView in memory. When a UIViewController is created, you can choose to initialize the view manually, allowing you to build the view hierarchy by hand, or create a nib file using Interface Builder. Both of these initializations, however, create a UIViewController with an associated view.

```
1  IBViewController *ib = [[IBViewController alloc]
                                    initWithNibName:@"IBViewController"
                                          bundle:nil];
2  ManualViewController *manual = [[ManualViewController alloc] init];
```

In the first line of code, we create a variable called ib from a custom UIViewController subclass named IBViewController. Here, we are initializing the view of ib using a nib named IBViewController.xib—notice the .xib file-extension is not needed in the initWithNibName method. In this case, the view associated with the view controller ib is loaded from the nib, IBViewController.xib.

In our second line of code, we create a variable named manual from a custom UIViewController subclass called ManualViewController. You'll notice in the second line of code that we just call the generic init function. Because we are not loading our view from a nib file, we'll need to manually create our view and view hierarchy in the loadView function of our ManualViewController class.

Developer Note

At the end of the day, you can either hand-code your UI or use the graphical user interface of Interface Builder to create nib files—both methods work perfectly well. On newer devices, performance is more or less the same; it just comes down to how you want to work. Naturally, writing code manually gives you more control and freedom than using Interface Builder, but doing so might take a little longer. Apple's Interface Builder User Guide is available at **fromideatoapp.com/reference#ib**. Interface Builder is a powerful tool that allows you to manage complicated connections between application objects. In the interest of space, however, this book does not cover the ins-and-outs of Interface Builder. Examples used throughout are shown using code samples, but nib files are also provided in downloadable code samples where appropriate.

iOS apps are not limited to one view controller; in fact, there are typi-cally multiple view controllers, each charged with managing the events that take place within the context of their UI. For example, visualize the iPhone's native iPod app.

When you launch the iPhone's native iPod app, there is one view controller that operates as the root view controller and manages the navigation of black tabs along the bottom of the screen. Each tab then contains another view controller that manages UITableViews and navi-gation within the context of that tab. When a new tab is selected, the root view controller decides which view to load next and then displays it to the user. Behind the scenes, iOS makes a series of calls to views that are about to be removed or shown on the screen.

Multiple View Controllers Managing Different Aspects of the iPod App's UI

View Life Cycle

What we just visualized with the iPhone's native iPod app is known as the view life cycle. The view life cycle is a series of events that are called in your UIViewController based on the state of your view, as shown in Table 5.1.

Method	Description
`viewDidLoad`	Called when the view of a UIViewController is first loaded into memory
`viewWillAppear:(BOOL)animated*`	Called just before the view of a UIViewController is shown or revealed on the screen
`viewDidAppear:(BOOL)animated*`	Called just after the view of a UIViewController is shown or revealed on the screen
`viewWillDisappear:(BOOL)animated*`	Called just before the view of a UIViewController is removed or hidden from the screen
`viewDidDisappear:(BOOL)animated*`	Called just after the view of a UIViewController is hidden or removed from the screen
`viewDidUnload`	Called when a view of a UIViewController has been unloaded from memory

*The animated Boolean indicates whether the view is being shown or hidden as part of an animation (e.g., sliding navigation).

If you override one of these methods in a custom UIViewController, it is very important that you call the same method on your superclass. For example, if you are overriding viewDidLoad, the first thing you should do is call [`super viewDidLoad`]. This lets iOS do any behind-the-scenes work it would normally take care of in viewDidLoad.

Get the Code ➡ ➡ ➡

Go to **fromideatoapp.com/download/example#viewlifecycle** to download an example project that demonstrates the various states of the view life cycle.

View Controllers, Navigation, and Modal Views

The UIViewController manages an associated view. Because we know that Model-View-Controller separates the actual user interface, it makes sense that the controllers handle the logic behind an app's navigation. If a view represents the canvas on which UI objects are placed, the controller represents the logic behind navigation from one view to the next.

We know that the UIViewController defines a basic interface for managing and interacting with UIView. Apple has made it easy to implement common navigation styles using subclasses of the UIViewController. These are the most common navigation styles:

- UITabBarController
- UINavigationController
- UISplitViewController
- UIPopoverController
- Modal Views

UITabBarController

The UITabBarController organizes a series of views into discrete sections that allow user input on a tab bar to navigate between each section. The UITabBarController's associated view consists of the tab bar interface and the content view of a selected tab.

Each UITabBarController also manages an array of view controllers. These managed view controllers represent the root view controller for content within a given tab. When a new tab is selected, the UITabBarController displays the content of the associated view controller and calls necessary view life cycle methods on other affected views (e.g., viewWillAppear, and viewWillDisappear).

The icon and text used to represent a view controller in the tab bar interface are configured in the root view controller for that tab. Essentially, when you create a new view controller, you define a property called the tabBarItem. When that view controller is loaded into the UITabBarController, the tab bar reflects the title and icon of tabBarItem set for the root view controller in that tab.

The following code block demonstrates how to create a new view controller, set up a tab bar item, and finally add the view controller as a tab to our UITabBarController.

```
1    //Create New View Controller
2    UIViewController *root = [[UIViewController alloc] init];
3
```

```
4    //Create a new UITabBarItem using the system item, Featured
5    UITabBarItem *tbi = [[UITabBarItem alloc]
                     initWithTabBarSystemItem:UITabBarSystemItemFeatured
                                          tag:0];
6
7    //Set our newly created UITabBarItem and clean up memory
8    root.tabBarItem = tbi;
9    [tbi release];
10
11   //Set our view controller as a tab in our UITabBarController
12   [tabBarController setViewControllers:[NSArray arrayWithObject:root]
                              animated:NO];
```

Designer Note

Notice in the previous code block that our **UITabBarItem** was created using a system default, **UITabBarSystemItemFeatured**. Apple has a series of system default items that define an icon image and text for common tabs such as Featured, Recent, Top Rated, and so on. If you use a system item, you cannot change the text or image. We will discuss all of the system buttons and how to create custom UITabBarItems in Chapter 7, Creating Custom Icons, Launch Images, and Buttons.

The iPhone's native clock app provides a great example of mixed view controllers presented using the UITabBarController.

Get the Code ➡ ➡ ➡

Go to **fromideatoapp.com/download/example#tabbarc** to download an example project that demonstrates the UITabBarController.

UINavigationController

The UINavigationController manages one of the most widely used navigation styles in iOS-based apps. This navigation style is the drill-down or sliding effect seen in the Mail, iPod, and Address Book apps. The UINavigationController consists of a navigation bar, a toolbar, a content view, and a navigation stack of each view controller in the navigation path from the root view controller.

The UINavigationController is kind of like UI on autopilot; iOS automatically handles many of the common functions. All you need to worry about is what is visible, and where you want to go next.

When you tell the UINavigationController where to go next, it automatically handles the sliding animation used to add or remove views from the screen and provide a Back button to navigate you back to where you were. It is helpful to visualize the UINavigationController as a stack of cards. When a new view is selected, it is simply placed on top of the stack, creating a small pile. You can easily get back to where you've been by removing cards from the top of the stack all the way back to the starting point.

Past View
Controllers
Represented
as a Stack in
the Navigation
Controller

In programming terms, adding and removing items from a stack is called pushing and popping, respectively. When a new view controller is added, that view controller is *pushed* onto the navigation stack. When a view controller is removed from the top of the stack by hitting the Back button, the view controller is *popped* from the navigation stack. The following code sample demonstrates how to animate a new view onto the screen using a UINavigationController.

```
1  DetailViewController *detail = [[DetailViewController alloc]
                                     initWithNibName:@"DetailView"
                                     bundle:nil];
2  [self.navigationController pushViewController:detail animated:YES];
3  [detail release];
```

As you can see in this code sample, we can drill down to the next level of our app with only a few lines of code. DetailViewController can be a completely separate set of UI, contained within a UIViewController as discussed previously. By pushing *detail* on the navigation stack, detail becomes the visible view controller and our current view controller animates off screen. In this case, our detail view controller pushes onto the stack using a sliding animation because we defined animated:YES; if we wanted the view controller to simply appear with no animation, we would set the animated Boolean parameter in line 2 to NO.

In our discussion of the view life cycle, the viewWillAppear, viewDidAppear, viewWillDisappear, and viewDidDisappear methods also had an animated property. In this case, because we are pushing *detail* on the screen with animation, its view life cycle methods also reflect an animation.

Tip

When we push a view controller onto the navigation stack, it increases the retain count by one, resulting in a retain count of two after line 2. Since we only need a reference to our detail view controller as long as it is in the navigation stack, we call a release to decrement the retain count in line 3. When the navigation controller is finished with our detail view controller, it calls a release resulting in a retain count of zero, which deallocates the variable from memory.

Get the Code ⇛ ⇛ ⇛

Go to **fromideatoapp.com/download/example#navc** to download an example project that demonstrates the UINavigationController.

UISplitViewController

The UISplitViewController is unique to the iPad. You cannot use a UISplitViewController on small screen iOS devices such as the iPhone or iPod touch. Like the UITabBarController, the UISplitViewController is a container for multiple view controllers; in this case there are two view controllers arranged side by side, left and right.

When an iPad is oriented in landscape mode, the UISplitView-Controller shows both view controllers. When the iPad is oriented in portrait mode, however, the UISplitViewController automatically hides the leftmost view controller and allows the rightmost view controller to occupy the entire screen.

Split View in Landscape and Portrait Modes

Delegate methods are provided that signal your app when such rotations occur. This allows you to add or remove buttons from your UI to account for the function that was just hidden or shown. From a UX standpoint, it is a bad idea to have commonly used functions such as primary navigation available only when your app is in a certain orientation.

```
1   // Called when a button should be added to a toolbar for a
2   // hidden view controller
3   - (void)splitViewController: (UISplitViewController*)svc
        willHideViewController: (UIViewController *)aViewController
            withBarButtonItem: (UIBarButtonItem*)barButtonItem
        forPopoverController: (UIPopoverController*)pc {
4
5       // Add your button for the newly hidden view controller
6
7   }
8
9   // Called when the view is shown again in the split view,
10  // invalidating the button and popover controller.
11  - (void)splitViewController: (UISplitViewController*)svc
        willShowViewController:(UIViewController *)aViewController
      invalidatingBarButtonItem:(UIBarButtonItem *)barButtonItem {
12
13      // Remove your button for the newly shown view controller
14
15  }
```

This long code block illustrates the two most important delegate methods for UISplitViewController. They look complicated, but if you read the functions as a sentence, what they are actually signaling becomes clear.

The first method (lines 3 through 7) is called when the iPad rotates to portrait, thus hiding the leftmost view controller in the UISplitViewController. Reading the function as a sentence, the split view controller, svc, hides the view controller aViewController. In doing so, the split view controller has prepared a bar button item, barButton Item, that when tapped displays the newly hidden view controller in the popover controller, pc. Using this information, we can add a button to the UI that shows the hidden view controller.

The second function (lines 11 through 15) demonstrates a scenario where the iPad is rotated to a landscape position, thus showing the hidden view controller. Again, reading this function as a sentence, our split view controller, svc, shows the view controller aViewController and invalidates the bar button item barButtonItem. Using this information, we can easily remove the barButtonItem from the UI.

Get the Code ⇒ ⇒ ⇒

Go to **fromideatoapp.com/download/example#svc** to download an example project that demonstrates the UISplitViewController.

UIPopoverController

We just talked about the UISplitViewController and you probably noticed in our code blocks references to something called a UIPopoverController. Like the UISplitViewController, the UIPopoverController is specific to the iPad and cannot be used on the iPhone or iPod touch. UIPopoverControllers are used to layer a new view controller on top of a visible view controller—a popover view. In a way, the UIPopoverController is much like a select-menu or drop-down menu on traditional HTML websites. But unlike websites, their content is not limited to a simple list, and as a designer or developer you can control the direction and behavior of the popover.

UIPopoverControllers are created, or initialized, with a root view controller. The UIPopoverController itself is not actually a subclass of UIViewController, but rather acts as a container object for layering a UIViewController on the screen. In the case of the UISplitViewController mentioned in the previous section, iOS automatically initialized our UIPopoverController with the view controller that was going to be hidden. From a UI standpoint, however, you can use UIPopoverControllers to layer any number of controls or UI objects contained in a UIViewController.

Popover Views

UIPopoverController

After initializing the UIPopoverController, you can configure it using the properties in Table 5.2.

TABLE 5.2
UIPopover-
Controller
Properties and
Descriptions

Property	Description
contentViewController	The view controller that will be displayed in the popover view
popoverContentSize	Of type CGSize(width, height), the popoverContentSize defines the height and width of the popover. This value defaults to the contentViewController contentPopoverSize if defined
passthroughViews	By default, if a user taps outside the popover view, the popover is hidden automatically. However, interaction with any views in the passthroughViews array will be ignored and will *not* dismiss the popover

Once you have created and configured the UIPopoverController, you can display it on the screen using one of two methods: presentPopover-FromRect or presentPopoverFromBarButtonItem. The following code sample demonstrates both methods. Here, the variable pop is a UIPop-overController that has already been initialized and configured.

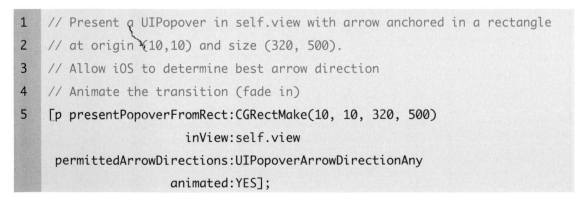

```
1   // Present a UIPopover in self.view with arrow anchored in a rectangle
2   // at origin (10,10) and size (320, 500).
3   // Allow iOS to determine best arrow direction
4   // Animate the transition (fade in)
5   [p presentPopoverFromRect:CGRectMake(10, 10, 320, 500)
                    inView:self.view
     permittedArrowDirections:UIPopoverArrowDirectionAny
                  animated:YES];
```

```
6
7    // Present a UIPopover with the arrow anchored from the left
8    // bar button item in our navigation controller.
9    // Allow all Arrow directions (iOS will determine most suitable)
10   // Animate the transition (fade in)
11   [p presentPopoverFromBarButtonItem:
                                 self.navigationItem.rightBarButtonItem
             permittedArrowDirections:UIPopoverArrowDirectionAny
                        animated:YES];
```

Tip

You can define multiple arrow directions using the | symbol. For example, if you want your popover to display either left or right, but not up or down, you can say permittedArrowDirections: UIPopoverArrow-DirectionLeft | UIPopoverArrowDirectionRight.

Get the Code ➠ ➠ ➠

Go to **fromideatoapp.com/download/example#svc** to download an example project that demonstrates the UIPopoverControllers and UISplitViewControllers.

Modal View Controllers

A modal view is one presented in front of another view (modally), usually to provide self-contained functions in a given workflow like content creation or special input. For example, when you are sending a text message on your iPhone, as you tap the camera icon to attach an image to your message, the camera or image picker slides up from the bottom as a modal view. Unlike a UIPopoverController, which is meant to be temporary or passive, a modal view takes center stage. On the iPad, when a modal view takes up less than the entire screen, touches or input with other views outside the bounds of modal view are ignored. Because modal views are designed to be self-contained tasks, you should give users a clear exit from the modal view either at the completion of the task (e.g., Send Email button) or with a Done or Cancel button.

When a user taps the Plus icon in the native iPhone calendar app, the new event dialog that slides from the bottom of the screen is presented as a modal view controller. Similarly, the compose new message dialog in the native Mail app on the iPad also uses a modal view. On the iPad, modal views can be configured to occupy only a portion of the screen while on the iPhone or iPod touch they must occupy the entire screen.

Unlike the view controllers we've talked about up to this point, a modal view controller is not a special subclass of UIViewController, but rather a relationship between two UIViewControllers. All properties of a modal view controller are defined in the UIViewController class. This means that any UIViewController can be presented as a modal view controller, and any UIViewController can present a modal view controller.

The View for Composing on the iPad Presented Modally

There are two crucial properties defined in a UIViewController that affect the modal view:

- modalTransitionStyle
- modalPresentationStyle

modalTransitionStyle

The modal transition style defines how the modal view will animate on the screen. If you present a modal view using `animated:NO` the modal transition style will have no effect. There are four possible modal transition styles:

- **UIModalTransitionStyleCoverVertical:** When presented, the modal view controller slides up from the bottom of the screen. When dismissed, the modal view controller slides down off the bottom of the screen. This is commonly used to compose emails or to create iPod playlists on the iPhone.

- **UIModalTransitionStyleFlipHorizontal:** When presented, the current view flips from right to left using 3D animation. The backside of the 3D animation flip is the modal view controller. When dismissed, the animation reverses left to right. This is most commonly used for info screens as seen in the native Weather app and Stocks app.

- **UIModalTransitionStyleCrossDissolve:** When presented, the modal view fades in on top of the current view. When dismissed, the animation reverses and the modal view fades out.

- **UIModalTransitionStylePartialCurl:** When presented, the bottom-right corner of the current view curls up like a piece of paper to reveal the modal view beneath. When the modal view is dismissed, the current view curls back down on top of the modal view.

modalPresentationStyle

Because of the small screen on the iPhone and iPod touch, different modal presentation styles are available only on the iPad. The modal presentation style defines how the modal view content view is displayed in the context of the entire screen. There are four possible modal presentation styles on the iPad:

- **UIModalPresentationFullScreen:** This is the default option for modal view presentation styles, and the only option for all iPhone and iPod modal views. Here, the modal view covers the entire screen at the end of the modal view transition.

- **UIModalPresentationPageSheet:** When a modal view is presented as a page sheet, the width of the content view is set to the width of the device in portrait mode or 768 points. When in landscape mode, the sheet is centered and the outlying areas are darkened. An example of this presentation style can be seen in the iPad's native Mail app by clicking the Compose New Message button.

- **UIModalPresentationFormSheet:** Like the page sheet presentation style, the form sheet modal view content view is smaller than the iPad's screen size and the area outside its bounds is darkened. However, the form sheet modal view presentation style has a fixed width and height of 540 points by 620 points, respectively. Rotating the device keeps the modal view centered on the screen without changing its size.

- **UIModalPresentationCurrentContext:** The modal view simply uses the same style as its parent view controller.

Get the Code ➡ ➡ ➡

Go to **fromideatoapp.com/download/example#modalview** to download an example project that demonstrates modal views, modal view transition styles, and modal view presentation styles.

CHAPTER 6

User Interface Buttons, Inputs, Indicators, and Controls

So far, we've been discussing the foundation that makes up basic iOS user interfaces. We've gone over physical hardware, we've learned about fundamental UI views, and we've discussed the importance of controllers and how to use controllers in applications. Now that we know where to put things and what to connect them to, it's time to discuss the actual control elements that come bundled with the iOS SDK.

This chapter is meant as a "kitchen-sink" or overview of all the system user interface elements available to you. Designers should pay close attention to how Apple defines the expected behavior and use of standard elements. Where appropriate, this chapter will outline the specific usage of system-provided UI elements as defined by the Human Interface Guidelines. Failure to follow these guidelines for system elements may result in rejection from the iTunes App Store.

We will cover how to customize UI elements in greater detail in Part III, Designing Custom iOS User Interface Objects.

Alert Dialogs and Action Sheets

Alert dialogs and action sheets are temporary views used to prompt the user for special input, or bring the user's attention to some detail. When an alert dialog or action sheet is visible, all other interaction with your app is disabled. Alert dialogs display in the center of the screen, and action sheets display as a row of buttons emerging from the bottom of the screen. iOS automatically animates the transition of these views on and off the screen.

Developer Note

UIAlertViews and UIActionSheets don't automatically dismiss when your apps enter background processing. If your app is running on a background-processing capable device, you should program-matically dismiss any UIAlertViews or UIActionSheets by imple-menting `applicationDidEnterBackground:(UIApplication *) application` in your app delegate.

Alert Dialog

An alert dialog, UIAlertView, prompts the user for more information about the current task or application. Alert dialogs consist of a title, a message body, and an array of buttons.

UIAlertView
Anatomy

1 Title

2 Message Body

3 Control Buttons

Remember that the UIAlertView interrupts the user's workflow with an intrusive dialog. For the best user experience, don't overuse UIAlertViews. They can be very useful for bringing a user's attention to information such as Internet connectivity or message prompts, but overusing alert dialogs will decrease their overall importance in your app and slow down workflows. Instead, try designing an elegant way to communicate the more general information to the user with on-screen UIViews.

> **Designer Note**
>
> You cannot modify the UIAlertView's look and feel or its position. The UIAlertView always appears at the center of the screen in the blue glass visual style that iOS users are accustomed to. This ensures consistency across the iOS platform, but presents a challenge to designers. If you need to communicate a simple message in dialog form and want it to match your application (such as downloading or connecting), consider designing a custom UIView overlay instead of using a UIAlertView.

Usage Guidelines

Generally speaking, when using UIAlertViews, you should follow the standards outlined in Apple's Human Interface Guidelines.

- **Title:** Titles should be short, descriptive, and often a sentence fragment. Avoid single-word titles as well as long sentence titles that take up more than one line. Finally, all titles should be succinct and in title-style capitalization, in which the first letter of most words is capitalized. Good examples include "New Text Message" or "No Internet Connection." Bad examples are "You have a new text message" or "There is no Internet connection."

- **Message Body:** The message body should be one or two lines long using sentence-style capitalization, where only the first word in each sentence is capitalized. If you have a long message, iOS automatically replaces the message body text label with a UIScrollView using black text on a white background. Scrolling alert views provide a poor user experience and should be avoided, so try to keep your messages short and to the point.

- **Buttons:** UIAlertViews have at least one button by default. Buttons can have two colors, light and dark. Always use verbs or action phrases—such as Reply, Cancel, or Add Contact—for button text. Avoid using Yes and No as options; use OK and Cancel instead.

The UIAlertView can have multiple buttons, but it requires at least one. Two buttons are preferred to give the user a choice between two mutually exclusive actions. Using more than two buttons can add unwanted complexity to your workflows, making it difficult for the user to read and respond to the information you are presenting.

Tip

If you need to give the user more than two options, consider using an action sheet, as described in the next section.

When presenting an alert view that performs a risky or destructive action, place a light-colored Cancel button on the right, and a dark-colored OK button on the left. If an alert view presents a positive action, place a light-colored OK button on the right and a dark-colored Cancel button on the left. This convention helps protect users from mistakenly choosing a destructive option if they don't read the dialog carefully.

Note

The button on the left is always dark-colored and represents a negative action like Log Off or Cancel. The button on the right is always light-colored and represents a positive action such as OK or Download.

Get the Code ⇒ ⇒ ⇒

Go to **fromideatoapp.com/download/example#kitchensink** to download an example project containing UIAlertViews.

Action Sheet

An action sheet presents the user with a set of visually stacked options, typically more than an alert view, with one button per row. Similar to the alert view, the action sheet on an iPhone and iPod touch overlays the top screen and blocks all other input. On the iPad however, action sheets display in the UIPopoverController mentioned in the previous chapter. Tapping outside the UIPopoverController simply dismisses the view.

Example Action Sheets on the iPhone (left) and iPad (right)

An action sheet consists of a title and an array of buttons. From this array of buttons, you have the option to define one button index that represents a cancel-like option, and one button index that represents a destructive option. The cancel-like option is dark gray, and the destructive option is red.

The overall style of the UIActionSheet can be configured using one of the following four options by setting the property actionSheetStyle:

- UIActionSheetStyleAutomatic
- UIActionSheetStyleDefault
- UIActionSheetStyleBlackTranslucent
- UIActionSheetStyleBlackOpaque

Guidelines
Action sheets direct user workflow. Alert views are typically informative, while action sheets provide options for completing a task.

When using action sheets on the iPhone, be sure to always present users with a cancel-like action. This is not always necessary on the iPad because tapping outside the bounds of the action sheet dismisses the UIPopoverController; on the iPhone, however, users do not have this option.

Note

It is possible to display an action sheet on the iPad within an existing UIPopoverController. In this case, the action sheet treats the popover controller's view much like an independent iPhone screen, sliding the action sheet from the bottom of the popover within the view. If you implement an action sheet in this way, be sure to present users with a cancel option.

Get the Code ⇒⇒⇒

Go to **fromideatoapp.com/download/example#kitchensink** to download an example project containing UIActionSheets.

Indicators

UIControls can be used to collect input, but they can also communicate information back to the user. Indicators provide feedback on progress or general information. Three indicators commonly used in iOS are shown in Table 6.1.

TABLE 6.1
Indicator Types

Indicator	Example
UIActivityIndicatorView	
UIProgressView	
UIPageControl	

UIActivityIndicatorView

More commonly known as a *spinner*, the UIActivityIndicatorView shows that your app is working on a process. Your app should never perform long tasks without providing some feedback to users. Using the UIActivityIndicatorView, you can automatically generate an iOS spinner in one of three styles:

- UIActivityIndicatorViewStyleWhiteLarge
- UIActivityIndicatorViewStyleWhite
- UIActivityIndicatorViewStyleGray

You can control your UIActivityIndicatorView using the startAnimating and stopAnimating functions.

```
1  UIActivityIndicatorView *spinner = [[UIActivityIndicatorView alloc]
       initWithActivityIndicatorStyle:UIActivityIndicatorViewStyleGray];
2  [self.view addSubview:spinner];
3  [spinner startAnimating];
4  /* perform some task that takes a long time */
5  [spinner stopAnimating];
```

Never show a UIActivityIndicatorView that is not animating because it signifies a stalled or stopped action to users. Note that the activity indicator does not show progress, but rather that some action is being performed (and that your app hasn't frozen). If your app is performing a predictable task and the feedback would be beneficial to users, consider using a progress view instead of an activity indicator view.

UIProgressView

The progress view, or progress bar, is a simple indicator that visualizes the amount of time elapsed and remaining on a given task. An example progress bar can be seen when downloading new mail messages from the native iOS Mail app.

There are two styles for the UIProgressView:

- **UIProgressViewStyleDefault**
- **UIProgressViewStyleBar**

UIPageControl

The page control shows the number of parallel screens, or pages, and the position of the selected screen. The UIPageControl is typically used in conjunction with a UIScrollView with the property pagingEnabled set to YES. An example of UIPageControl is seen in the native iOS Weather application. The UIPageControl is configured simply by defining the number of pages and the current page.

UIPageControl
Examples

Controls and Buttons

UIControl is a special subclass of UIView. The UIControl class defines the basic interaction you would expect from UI elements such as buttons and sliders. Each UIControl item can have a target action for a specified event. UIControls can respond to UIControlEvents defined as

- UIControlEventTouchDown
- UIControlEventTouchDownRepeat
- UIControlEventTouchDragInside
- UIControlEventTouchDragOutside
- UIControlEventTouchDragEnter
- UIControlEventTouchDragExit
- UIControlEventTouchUpInside
- UIControlEventTouchUpOutside
- UIControlEventTouchCancel
- UIControlEventValueChanged
- UIControlEventEditingDidBegin
- UIControlEventEditingChanged
- UIControlEventEditingDidEnd
- UIControlEventEditingDidEndOnExit

Note

When building your apps, put the target actions for specified events of UIControls in the UIViewController class that is associated with the UIControl's parent view. This helps ensure the Model-View-Controller architecture and keeps your code modular if you ever need to make changes down the road.

Get the Code ⇒ ⇒ ⇒

Go to **fromideatoapp.com/download/example#kitchensink** to download an example project that contains all of the UIControl examples seen in the following sections.

System-Provided Buttons

Apple has created various default button styles to represent common UI tasks. These button styles can easily be used in tab bars, toolbars, or navigation bars. Using a system-provided button style can speed up your development time, and provide consistency across multiple iOS applications. However, if you use a system-provided button to represent an action other than its original intention, your app may be rejected for violating Apple's Human Interface Guidelines.

Apple does not directly provide you with the image assets used in system-provided button styles. Instead, button creation methods in the API allow you to design buttons using a button style constant. For example, consider the following code block:

```
1   UITabBarItem *t = [[UITabBarItem alloc]
        initWithTabBarSystemItem:UITabBarSystemItemSearch tag:0];
```

In this code example, we create a new UITabBarItem with the system UITabBarItem style, UITabBarSystemItemSearch.

System-Provided Toolbar Buttons

Table 6.2 describes the system-provided toolbar buttons available in iOS. Remember to use them only according to the meaning specified. Most system-provided toolbar buttons can have a plain style, or be styled with a border.

Plain Style vs. Border Style Toolbar Buttons

TABLE 6.2 System-Provided Toolbar Buttons

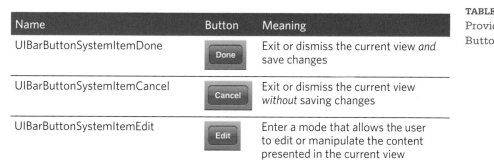

Name	Button	Meaning
UIBarButtonSystemItemDone	Done	Exit or dismiss the current view *and* save changes
UIBarButtonSystemItemCancel	Cancel	Exit or dismiss the current view *without* saving changes
UIBarButtonSystemItemEdit	Edit	Enter a mode that allows the user to edit or manipulate the content presented in the current view

continues

TABLE 6.2
continued

Name	Button	Meaning
UIBarButtonSystemItemSave	Save	Save changes and end editing mode of the current view. Do not use the Save button to dismiss a view; instead, use the Done button style
UIBarButtonSystemItemUndo	Undo	Undo the most recent action (available since iOS 3.0)
UIBarButtonSystemItemRedo	Redo	Redo the most recent undone action (available since iOS 3.0)
UIBarButtonSystemItemPageCurl		Trigger a page curl animation on the current view such as in the native Maps app. Do not use this button style to trigger any other animation style, e.g., flip animation
UIBarButtonSystemItemCompose		Present a new view or action sheet for composing a new message
UIBarButtonSystemItemReply		Present a new view or action sheet for responding or routing to the object on screen
UIBarButtonSystemItemAction		Open an action sheet that presents the user with application-specific actions
UIBarButtonSystemItemOrganize		Move or route an item to a new location, such as moving email messages in an inbox
UIBarButtonSystemItemBookmarks		Show bookmarks specific to your app
UIBarButtonSystemItemSearch		Open or present a search related view
UIBarButtonSystemItemRefresh		Reload the information in the current view
UIBarButtonSystemItemStop		Stop the current process or task on screen or in the background
UIBarButtonSystemItemCamera		Open an action sheet that displays the standard photo picker in camera mode (allowing pictures to be taken)
UIBarButtonSystemItemTrash		Delete or remove the current item from the context of the current view
UIBarButtonSystemItemPlay		Begin playback
UIBarButtonSystemItemPause		Pause playback

Name	Button	Meaning
UIBarButtonSystemItemRewind		Rewind media playback
UIBarButtonSystemItemFastForward		Fast-forward media playback

System-Provided Tab Bar Buttons

Table 6.3 represents system-provided tab bar buttons available in iOS. Remember to use them only according to the meaning specified.

Name	Button	Meaning
UITabBarSystemItemMore	More	Show additional tab bar items. iOS automatically includes a More tab when there are more than five UITabBarItems in a UITabBarController
UITabBarSystemItemFavorites	Favorites	Show user-determined favorites
UITabBarSystemItemFeatured	Featured	Show app-specific featured items
UITabBarSystemItemTopRated	Top Rated	Show app-specific top-rated items
UITabBarSystemItemRecents	Recents	Show most recent item or recent actions taken by user
UITabBarSystemItemContacts	Contacts	Show contacts, either local to your app or provide access to the user's iOS address book
UITabBarSystemItemHistory	History	Show a list of actions or steps taken by the user
UITabBarSystemItemBookmarks	Bookmarks	Show app-specific bookmarks
UITabBarSystemItemSearch	Search	Show a search view of your app
UITabBarSystemItemDownloads	Downloads	Show recent or active app-specific downloads
UITabBarSystemItemMostRecent	Most Recent	Show the most recent item
UITabBarSystemItemMostViewed	Most Viewed	Show the most popular item for all users of your app

TABLE 6.3 System-Provided Tab Bar Buttons

Note

Use UI elements consistently throughout your app. This not only improves the user experience across applications you design and develop, but also improves the overall user experiences across iOS. For more information about the importance of using UI elements consistently, go to **fromideatoapp.com/reference#consistent** and refer to Apple's Human Interface Guidelines.

UIButton

The UIButton is the simplest implementation of a UIControl. Essentially, the UIButton turns a rectangular area (defined in the UIView superclass) and assigns it a target action based on a UIControlEvent. There are four primary button types: Rounded Rectangle, Info, Detail Disclosure, and Add Contact. A fifth type, called a Custom button, UIButtonTypeCustom, creates a button with no type or style assumptions, allowing you to design your own custom buttons.

Note

We will cover how to create custom buttons in Chapter 7, Creating Custom Icons, Launch Images, and Buttons.

Rounded Rectangle Button

The Rounded Rectangle button, UIButtonTypeRoundedRect, is most commonly seen in the iPhone's native Address Book app. Buttons created using this style come preloaded with a UILabel subview identified as the title property for the button. This UILabel is centered and has a bold system font with a dark blue color.

Rounded Rectangle Button Transitioning from Normal to Selected State

Developer Note

When setting properties for a rectangle button such as the title label, use the UIControl interface functions, setTitle:(NSString*) title forState:(UIControlState)state, setImage:(UIImage*)image forState:(UIControlState)state, etc. To set the default value, use the control state, UIControlStateNormal.

> **Designer Note**
>
> When designing buttons, you have the option to design text
> and style options for the various UIControlStates available. You can
> design buttons that take advantage of normal, highlighted, selected,
> and disabled states.

Info Button

The Info button is used to display detailed information, options, or configurations for an app or view. Often, the Info button uses a flip animation to reveal the options behind a given view. You can choose to use a
light or dark Info button, but you cannot set a title.

Info Button in
Weather App

Detail Disclosure Button

The Detail Disclosure button is used to reveal more information about
a given topic. This is most commonly seen in the iPhone's native recent
calls list, or on the iPhone's native Maps app.

In the iPhone's native Phone app, selecting a row on the recent calls list
calls that number; however, when you hit the Detail Disclosure button,
it will instead drill-down and reveal more information about that call.

Detail Disclose
Button in
UITableViewCell

Contact Add

The Contact Add button, most commonly seen on the right side of the
"To:" field when composing an email, presents the user with an address
book interface for selecting contacts.

Contact Add
Button in Compose
Email Message
Modal View

Picker

A picker, or UIPickerView, allows users to select a value from an arbitrary list. Characterized by the slot-machine-style wheel, list items scroll up and down within the list. UIPickers have a fixed height and width and should always be designed to fill the lower portion of the screen. For the iPad, consider placing a UIPicker in a UIPopoverController if necessary.

> **Developer Note**
>
> You can define the number of "wheels" in the UIPickerView by implementing numberOfComponentsInPickerView: and pickerView:numberOfRowsInComponent in the UIPickerView's datasource. The delegate and datasource of a UIPickerView work similar to the UITableView. When the UIPickerView updates a row, it calls pickerView:titleForRow:forComponent: in the delegate function.

Date and Time Picker

The date and time picker, or UIDatePicker, is a special instance of the UIPicker class. Here, the UIPicker is specifically designed for selecting date and time values. You can configure a UIDatePicker to operate under one of four UIDatePickerModes:

- **Time:** Select hours, minutes, and optionally AM/PM (e.g., 2:45 AM).

- **Date:** Select month, day, and year (e.g., February 5, 2011).

- **Date and Time:** Select day, hour, year, and optionally AM/PM (e.g., Today, 2:45 AM)

- **Countdown Timer:** Select an hour and minute value (e.g., 3 hours 50 min).

Note

All date and time picker modes automatically reflect a user's local date format preferences.

Segmented Control

A segmented control is a radio style selector, similar to the UITabBar-Controller, which defines a group of buttons and a selected index. The number of segments and their relative size determines the width of a segmented control. Additionally, the height of a segmented control is fixed. You can style the segmented control by choosing from one of four UISegmentControlStyles, or by defining the tintColor property where available:

- **UISegmentedControlStylePlain:** The default segmented control style.

- **UISegmentedControlStyleBordered:** A large, bordered, segmented control style.

- **UISegmentedControlStyleBar:** A smaller, segmented control style typically used when the segmented control is added to a UIToolbar. This style can be tinted using the tintColor property.

- **UISegmentedControlStyleBezeled:** A large, bezeled style. This style can be tinted using the tintColor property.

Switch

A switch, or UISwitch, is used to control Boolean-based options. A switch must be either on or off, but cannot be both. The text for a UISwitch always says On or Off and cannot be changed. When a user "flips" the switch, it responds to the UIControlEvent, UIControlEventValueChanged.

Example of
UISwitches

Slider

The slider, or UISlider, is used to input a single value within a range of values. Much like a switch, when a slider moves it responds to the UIControlEvent, UIControlEventValueChanged, giving you the ability to manipulate the slider's effect in real time. A common example of the UISlider can be found on the brightness setting for any iOS device.

Example of a UISlider

Tip

If you do not need to update your app in real time based on the slider's position (e.g., a slider used to control difficulty in a game), you can set the property continuous to NO, which causes the UISlider to signal UIControlEventValueChanged only when the slider stops moving.

Text Field

A text field, or UITextField, is used to accept a single line of keyboard text from the user. Along with font size and color, you can style your UITextField by selecting from one of four border styles including: UITextBorderStyleNone, UITextBorderStyleLine, UITextBorderStyle-Bezel, UITextBorderStyleRoundedRect.

Tip

Use the hintText property to pre-populate the text field with some default value or example text using a light gray font. When the user taps the field, this text automatically disappears.

Additionally, when a user taps on the UITextField, a keyboard automatically displays on the screen. To improve the user experience, you can configure the style of keyboard displayed for each UITextField:

- UIKeyboardTypeDefault
- UIKeyboardTypeASCIICapable
- UIKeyboardTypeNumbersAndPunctuation
- UIKeyboardTypeURL
- UIKeyboardTypeNumberPad
- UIKeyboardTypePhonePad
- UIKeyboardTypeNamePhonePad
- UIKeyboardTypeEmailAddress

Various Keyboard Styles

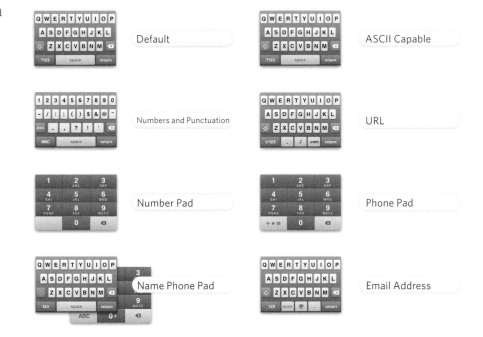

iOS App Blueprint

The Basics

In the previous blueprint, we started a sample project called "Hello, World!" That walkthrough was meant to make you comfortable with creating and setting up a new iOS project in Xcode. Now we'll create a new project that we'll use from here on. Using the steps you learned in the "Hello, World!" blueprint, open a new window-based project and name it "FI2ADemo."

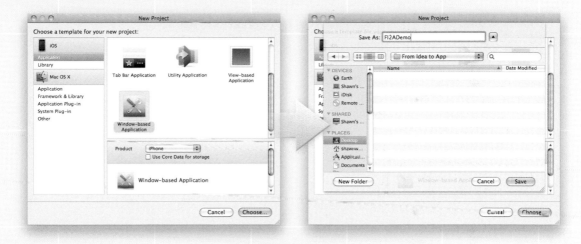

In this blueprint, we'll create two different UIViewControllers based on the different subclasses we have learned. Specifically, we'll set up a UITabBarController with two tabs, each with its own set of UI elements. Doing this requires the following steps:

1. Set up a UIViewController for each of the two tabs.
2. Add our unique UI elements to each UIViewController.
3. Connect the UI controls to a controller.
4. Create a UITabBarController using our two UIViewControllers as tabs.

Creating UIViewControllers

The first thing to do is to set up a UIViewController for each tab. Just as we did in the previous blueprint, we're going to add our code to the applicationDidFinishLaunching method of our app delegate. In this case, the app delegate is named FI2ADemoAppDelegate.m.

The following code block will create two UIViewControllers (one for each tab) and set the background color of their associated views to different colors (so we know when the tab is changed). Remember that the UITabBarController references each view controller for the UITabBarItem (our tab icon and text). When we set up the UIViewControllers, we'll also set their tab icons as a system icon style.

```
1   // Create the first view controller as tab1
2   // Set the background color of tab1 to light gray
3   UIViewController *tab1 = [[UIViewController alloc]
       initWithNibName:nil bundle:nil];
4   tab1.view.backgroundColor = [UIColor lightGrayColor];
5
6   // Create a new tab bar item (UITabBarController icon)
7   //     using the system icon style "featured"
8   // Set the new tab bar item to tab 1
9   // Clean up memory, we don't need tbi1 anymore
10  UITabBarItem *tbi1 = [[UITabBarItem alloc]
       initWithTabBarSystemItem:UITabBarSystemItemFeatured
       tag:0];
11  [tab1 setTabBarItem:tbi1];
12  [tbi1 release];
13
14  // Create the second view controller as tab2
15  UIViewController *tab2 = [[UIViewController alloc]
       initWithNibName:nil bundle:nil];
16
```

```
17  // Create a new tab bar item (UITabBarController icon)
18  //     using the system icon style "favorites"
19  // Set the new tab bar item to tab 2
20  // Clean up memory, we don't need tbi2 anymore
21  UITabBarItem *tbi2 = [[UITabBarItem alloc]
        initWithTabBarSystemItem:UITabBarSystemItemFavorites tag:0];
22  [tab2 setTabBarItem:tbi2];
23  [tbi2 release];
```

Adding UIControls to Each Tab

In Part II, The Basics of iOS User Interfaces, we learned about view
hierarchy and how to add UIViews as subviews. Eventually, the views
of the UIViewControllers we just created will be added as subviews to
the UITabBarController. But first, we want to add some UI elements
to those views themselves.

In Chapter 6, User Interface Buttons, Inputs, Indicators, and Controls,
we learned about the different UI elements in iOS that facilitate user
input and feedback. The first thing we need to do is set up some controls in our FI2ADemoAppDelegate.h files so we can reference them
later in our controller method.

```
1   #import <UIKit/UIKit.h>
2
3   @interface FI2ADemoAppDelegate : NSObject <UIApplicationDelegate> {
4       UIWindow *window;
5       UITextField *input;
6       UILabel *label1;
7   }
8
9   @property(nonatomic,retain) IBOutlet UIWindow *window;
10
11  @end
```

Lines 5 and 6 add two new objects to our app delegate, a UITextField named input, and a UILabel named label1. We'll reference these objects from the controller method.

The following code block will create and add a text field, button, and label to our first tab. We'll connect these UI elements to our controller later; for now, we'll just add them as a subview to our first tab's view.

```
1   // Create a UITextField input with frame (x,y,width,height)
2   // Set text field border style to Rounded Rect
3   // Add our text field to tab1's view
4   input = [[UITextField alloc]
            initWithFrame:CGRectMake(20, 20, 280, 30)];
5   input.borderStyle = UITextBorderStyleRoundedRect;
6   [tab1.view addSubview:input];
7
8   // Create a button with type Rounded Rect
9   // Set the frame of our button (x,y,width,height)
10  // Set the text of our button for control state normal
11  // Add our button to tab1's view
12  UIButton *button = [UIButton buttonWithType:UIButtonTypeRoundedRect];
13  button.frame = CGRectMake(20, 70, 280, 40);
14  [button setTitle:@"Set Text" forState:UIControlStateNormal];
16  [tab1.view addSubview:button];
17
18  // Create a label with frame (x,y,width,height)
19  // Set the text alignment of our label to "center"
20  // Add our label to tab1's view
21  label1 = [[UILabel alloc]
            initWithFrame:CGRectMake(20, 120, 280, 40)];
22  label1.textAlignment = UITextAlignmentCenter;
23  [tab1.view addSubview:label1];
```

Next, we will add a spinner (UIActivityViewIndicator) and a label (UILabel) to our second tab. As in the code block above, we'll create the variables and then add them as subviews of tab2's view.

```
1    // Create a spinner using the "large white" style
2    // Set the center of our spinner to the center of tab2's view,
3    //   this will position the spinner in the center of the screen
4    // Start the spinner animation (make it spin)
5    // Add the spinner as a subview to tab2
6    UIActivityIndicatorView *spin = [[UIActivityIndicatorView alloc]
         initWithActivityIndicatorStyle:
            UIActivityIndicatorViewStyleWhiteLarge];
7    spin.center = tab2.view.center;
8    [spin startAnimating];
9    [tab2.view addSubview:spin];
10
11   // Create a label with frame (x,y,width,height)
12   // Set the text alignment of our label to "center"
13   // Add our label to tab1's view
14   UILabel *label2 = [[UILabel alloc]
         initWithFrame:CGRectMake(20, 280, 280, 40)];
15   label2.textAlignment = UITextAlignmentCenter;
16   label2.text = @"Loading...";
17   [tab2.view addSubview:label2];
```

Note

If you ran your project at this point, you'd simply see a white screen. Even though we've created our view controllers and added UI elements as subviews to those view controllers' views, we haven't yet added any subviews to our main window.

Connecting UI Controls to a Controller

In the first tab we have a text field, a button, and a label. We want to make it so that when a user presses the button, the value of the text field is set to the value of the label.

One of the benefits of working with iOS is the ability to subclass standard classes, thus creating custom versions. Keeping in mind our Model-View-Controller design paradigm, this allows us to isolate the controllers to their respective views. In our case, we can isolate the controllers for each tab to the tab itself.

We haven't quite learned how to customize a UIViewController yet, however. So right now the only controller we can connect our UI elements to is the app delegate. (We'll learn how to subclass UIViewController in Part III, Designing Custom iOS User Interface Objects.) To use our delegate as the controller for the button, we add an action to the button setting the target of the action as "self." Since this is implemented in the app delegate, "self" means that when the button is pressed, iOS will call the action method on our app delegate.

We start by declaring our method in the app delegate header file (FI2ADemoAppDelegate.h), just after the window property declaration.

```
1   #import <UIKit/UIKit.h>
2   @interface FI2ADemoAppDelegate : NSObject <UIApplicationDelegate> {
3       UIWindow *window;
4       UITextField *input;
5       UILabel *label1;
6   }
7
8   @property(nonatomic,retain) IBOutlet UIWindow *window;
9
10  // Declare our button pressed method
11  - (void)changeText:(id)sender;
12
13  @end
```

This code block is an example of our FI2ADemoAppDelegate.h file. Notice that in line 11 we declared a new method, changeText, with the parameter sender. This is the method we'll define as our action for pressing the button.

Next, in our FI2ADemoAppDelegate.m file, we tell the button what action to call when pressed. This is simply one line of code:

```
1  // Add an action to our button
2  //   - Set the target to self, this is where
3  //     we implement the action
4  //   - Set the action to call method changeText:
5  //   - Call the action for event "touch up inside"
6  //     (call when the finger lifts up on the button)
7  [button addTarget:self
             action:@selector(changeText:)
      forControlEvents:UIControlEventTouchUpInside];
```

Finally, we implement the changeText method in the app delegate. Remember, we want this method to take the text from our text field and set it to the text of our label. Unlike our previous code changes, this change is made outside the applicationDidLaunch method. Add the following code block to the FI2ADemoAppDelegate.m file after the right brace (}) of the applicationDidLaunch method.

```
1  - (void)changeText:(id)sender{
2      label1.text = input.text;
3      [input endEditing:YES];
4  }
```

When the button is pressed, the changeText method is called. We simply take the value of input and assign it as the value of label1. In line 3, we tell input to end editing, which dismisses our keyboard.

Create a UITabBarController

We've created UIViewControllers, added UI elements, and set up those elements to controller methods. Since the icons for view controllers in the tab bar are defined in the view controllers, now we simply have to create our tab bar and add its view to the main window.

```
1  // Create a new tab bar controller
2  // Set the view controllers of the tab bar controller
3  //   to our view controllers, tab1 and tab2
4  // Add the view of our tab bar controller as a subview
5  //   to our main window
6  UITabBarController *tabBar = [[UITabBarController alloc]
      initWithNibName:nil bundle:nil];
7  [tabBar setViewControllers:
      [NSArray arrayWithObjects:tab1,tab2,nil]];
8  [self.window addSubview:tabBar.view];
```

And that's it! To run the project, click the Build and Run button in Xcode, or choose *Build > Build and Run* from the Xcode menu.

Get the Code ➡ ➡ ➡

Go to **fromideatoapp.com/downloads/blueprints** to download FI2ADemo and all of the project files.

PART III

Designing Custom iOS User Interface Objects

CHAPTER 7

Creating Custom Icons, Launch Images, and Buttons

Every app should have at least some custom artwork. This is actually one of the principles found in Apple's Human Interface Guidelines. One of the key factors in creating a positive user experience is the impact of high quality graphics. Sure, you can get away with using system provided buttons and controls, but by creating your own image assets and leveraging the power of iOS, you can not only make a great app, but also make it your own.

Apple has created a remarkable foundation for custom iOS user interfaces. Up to this point we've learned about various system inputs, buttons, and controls. Now we'll learn how to customize iOS UI elements and create superlative, five-star apps. In the last chapter, we covered all of the system-provided buttons and controls. Here we'll focus on creating app icons, launch images, and buttons using system-provided API methods in iOS. We'll discuss file types and sizes needed for creating these UI elements; however, you will need to prepare your image assets.

App Icons

App icons have become an important part of the iOS ecosystem. Your icon will represent your app in the iTunes App Store and will identify your app on an iOS device. We've all scanned through screens of icons looking for a particular app that eludes us, trying to remember what the icon looks like. Users will come to know your app by its icon—it is essentially your app's primary branding medium—so it's important that you put some time and thought into how to best represent your app.

App Icon in iTunes and on iPhone

App icons should be simple yet creative. Your icon is your app's first impression to new users, so consider quality and consistency when choosing imagery to represent your app. When designing your app icon, do not include the price, or words like "free" or "sale." Where appropriate, you may use the word "lite" to identify limited-featured apps.

Note

While not required for iOS development, it is recommended that you have access to photo editing software such as Adobe Photoshop or Gimp to create high-quality image assets for your apps. Go to **fromideatoapp. com** to download image assets used as examples in this book. And check out **peachpit.com** for training books or **kelbytraining.com,** the online training site Kelby Training for more advanced image-creation training.

App Icon Specifications

Your app icon will appear in two places on an iOS device: on the home screen, where it is used to launch the app; and when your app comes up in iOS Spotlight search results. When building your app, it is best to provide a separate icon file optimized for each of these scenarios.

Apple recommends using PNG files (.png) for all icon images. Additionally, your app icon must have 90-degree corners to form a square image, and may not use any transparency. Table 7.1 shows sizes and naming conventions for iOS icons.

TABLE 7.1 App Icon Sizes

Scenario	Size (pixels)	Naming Convention	Example
Default*	57 x 57	Icon.png	PSW
Default Search	29 x 29	Icon-Small.png	PSW
Retina Display	114 x 114	Icon@2x.png	PSW
Retina Display Search	58 x 58	Icon-Small@2x.png	PSW
iPad	72 x 72	Icon-72.png	PSW
iPad Search	50 x 50	Icon-Small-50.png	PSW

*Denotes a required icon. All other icons are recommended given that your app will operate on the corresponding hardware configurations.

When you upload your app to iTunes Connect, the service used to manage your apps in the iTunes App Store, you'll also need to provide a high-resolution (512 x 512) app icon image file. Apple will use this high-resolution version to represent your app in iTunes and the iTunes App Store. For this reason, it is best to design your app icons at the larger 512 x 512 resolution and then scale down to create new files for each icon version as needed.

Note

The app icon images don't have to be exactly the same for each use, but they should be similar. For example, if your app file is universal, meaning it will run optimized on both an iPhone and an iPad, you can use a slightly different icon for each device. You should not, however, change the icon significantly. Doing so may result in rejection from the iTunes App Store for violating the Human Interface Guidelines.

Designer Note

Because making multiple icon files is such a common task, I've created a Photoshop action that automatically creates all six icon sizes (naming them accordingly) based on a single 512 x 512 master icon file. Go to **fromideatoapp.com/downloads#PSactions** to download this and other Photoshop action scripts used in iOS design.

Notice how the app icons in the previous examples all have squared edges and do not have the gloss bevel effect characteristic of iOS app icons. When designing your app icons, it is important that you *do not add these effects*. iOS automatically adds the rounded corners and glossed bevel effect to your app icons, thus keeping them consistent across all apps in the App Store.

Developer Note

When configuring your app's info property list file (.plist), you have the option of adding the value "Icon already includes gloss effects". If you set this value to true, iOS will not add the traditional glossed bevel seen on most app icons. This can be useful for app icon designs that do not need the glossed bevel such as the iPhone's native Settings app, Maps app, or Calendar app.

Launch Images

We live in a world of first impressions. Users will form an opinion about your app within the first seconds. When a user begins to use your app, the first thing they are presented with, while the app loads, is the *launch image.* Users are typically eager to dive in, so be aware that the image can feel like a barrier. It's also an opportunity to introduce your application each time—and this time you have many more pixels than you did for the icon!

This is especially true if your app is free. Free apps have a tendency to be deleted more quickly than paid apps because the user is willing to just try an app—no financial commitment. If they don't like it, they know they can delete it without wasting any money. With paid apps, people are usually more willing to give your app a chance after they've paid. So considering this, it is important to grab your user's attention with an appropriate launch image.

What's happening behind the scenes is that as an app launches, iOS temporarily displays the launch image as defined by your app's info property list file (.plist). From a technical standpoint, this is done so that users have immediate feedback that your app has launched while iOS loads necessary resources in the background. Once these resources have been loaded, the launch image disappears and your UI is shown.

As with app icons, you have the option of defining multiple launch images based on different launch conditions (see Table 7.2). On the iPhone, you can define a separate launch image for the standard iPhone display, or the retina display. For the iPad, you can define different launch images based on the orientation of the device. (Orientation-specific launch images are not available on iPhone as of iOS 4.2.)

Use case	Size (pixels)	Naming Convention
Default	320 x 480	Default.png
Retina display	640 x 960	Default@2x.png
iPad portrait	768 x 1004	Default-Portrait~ipad.png
iPad landscape	1024 x 748	Default-Landscape~ipad.png

TABLE 7.2
Launch Image
Specifications

Note

The launch image naming convention also supports LandscapeLeft and LandscapeRight accordingly. In general, [filename]-[orientation]-[scale]~[device].png is the naming convention.

Launch Images
in Landscape and
Portrait on the iPad

Custom UI Buttons

Part of designing your own user experience involves developing a unique feel to your app—in order to develop this feeling, you need to start with customized UI elements.

There are three primary classes of buttons you will come across when creating custom iOS UI elements: UITabBarItem, UIBarButtonItem, and UIButton. We've discussed how to use system default styles for these buttons, but now we'll cover how to create your own custom buttons using images and text.

When creating custom buttons, remember to be consistent across your app. Because you will likely be mixing custom UI with system UI, you should use the same font styles and shadow light sources as in the system elements.

In general, your custom UI should consider the following guidelines:

- Assume a top-down light source. Shadows and gradients should behave as if there is a light source at the top (90 degrees) of the screen.

- Choose the font Helvetica, which is the default typeface in iOS UI elements.

- Do not use imagery that could be easily mistaken for a system-provided button style.

- Because your app will likely be viewed on both standard and high-resolution retina displays, provide two image assets using the naming conventions discussed in Chapter 3, Physical Hardware.

UITabBarItem

UITabBarItems are used to identify a section in the UITabBarController, as discussed previously in Chapter 5, User Interface Controllers and Navigation. When using a system UITabBarItem, you'll notice a consistent white-to-gray gradient when the tab is not selected, and a white-to-blue gradient when the tab is selected. You should mimic this style when creating a custom UITabBarItem. Fortunately, doing so is remarkably simple.

The UITabBarItem can be initialized with a custom image and title. When loaded into a UITabBarController, the UITabBarItem registers only the alpha component of your image and automatically overlays the gradients you see in the system-provided buttons. This means that when designing a custom UITabBarItem, you only need to create a solid color transparent PNG of the silhouette of your button image. UITabBarItem images should be approximately 30 x 30 for standard-resolution displays, and 60 x 60 for high-resolution retina displays. Selected and not selected states handle automatically.

PNG with Transparency (left) Used for UITabBarItem Image (right).

The following code sample creates a custom UITabBarImage using an image named "homescreen" and gives it the label "Home". This assumes our app bundle contains both homescreen.png and homescreen@2x.png.

```
1    UITabBarItem *b = [[UITabBarItem alloc] initWithTitle:@"Home"
                                              image:@"homescreen"
                                              tag:0];
```

Tip

In iOS 4.0 and later, it is not necessary to include the .png file extension in the image parameter; in earlier versions of iOS, however, you must include the full file name, homescreen.png.

Get the Code ⇒ ⇒ ⇒

Go to **fromideatoapp.com/downloads/example#buttons** to download Custom Buttons and all of the project files.

UIBarButtonItem

The UIBarButtonItem is a special button class designed to work specifically with toolbars and navigation bars. You can create a custom UIBarButtonItem using static text, an image, or a custom UIView. You also have the option of defining the button style, which can either be UIBarButtonItemStylePlain, UIBarButtonItemStyleBordered, or UIBarButtonItemStyleDone.

UIBarButtonItems can be added only to toolbars and navigation bars. On the iPhone and iPad, these buttons are approximately 20 pixels tall with a varying width (depending on your button's needs). On the retina display, these buttons are approximately 40 pixels tall. Both the plain style and the bordered style automatically inherit the tint color of the toolbar or navigation bar they are added to.

Look at the following code sample. Here we create two different UIBarButtonItems. The first button created uses a bordered button style and is initialized with the text "Settings". The second button is created using the plain style and initialized with an image called "gear.png".

```
1   UIBarButtonItem *b1 = [[UIBarButtonItem alloc] initWithTitle:@"Settings"
        style:UIBarButtonItemStyleBordered
      target:self
      action:@selector(settingsPressed:)];
2   UIBarButtonItem *b2 = [[UIBarButtonItem alloc] initWithImage:@"gear.png"
        style:UIBarButtonItemStylePlain
      target:self
      action:@selector(settingsPressed:)];
```

Get the Code ➡ ➡ ➡

Go to **fromideatoapp.com/downloads/example#buttons** to download
Custom Buttons and all of the project files.

UIButton

We know from Chapter 6, User Interface Buttons, Inputs, Indicators,
and Controls, that there are different types of UIButtons: Info, Add
Contact, Rounded Rectangle, and so on. When using the Info and Add
Contact system button styles, you have no options for further customization. The Rounded Rectangle and custom styles, however, let you
create Custom buttons as needed.

Remember that UIButtons are a subclass of UIControl. This means
that they respond to the various UIControlStates:

- UIControlStateNormal
- UIControlStateHighlighted
- UIControlStateDisabled
- UIControlStateSelected

When you create custom UIButtons, you set properties like text,
images, and backgrounds for different UIControlStates. These prop
erties are set using the interface methods for the UIButton class
described in Table 7.3.

Method	Description
setTitle:forState:	Set the text value of the button for a given UIControlState
setTitleColor:forState:	Set the text color of the button for a given UIControlState
setTitleShadowColor:forState:	Set the text shadow color of the button for a given UIControlState
setBackgroundImage:forState:	Set the background image of the button for a given UIControlState
setImage:forState:	Set the button image for a given UIControlState

TABLE 7.3 UIButton
Class Interface
Methods

At the end of the day, creating custom UI elements on a mobile device is about efficiency—you really don't have a lot of extra room for wasted resources. Instead of creating an image for each button, design one image that can be used as a background and then simply change the text using the setTitle method in iOS. If your button is just text, consider using the default or slightly modified rounded rectangle style. This will help make your app consistent with other iOS apps. If you want to make a button from an image, similar to the Info or Add Contact buttons, use the custom style, which creates buttons with a transparent background.

Tip

You do not need to create a "button down" state for buttons that have an image background. iOS automatically overlays a semitransparent black layer on top of your button, indicating that it is pressed.

Rounded Rectangle Button

Rounded Rectangle buttons can be used to create quick, iOS-styled buttons with a custom font, text, and image treatments. By default, these buttons have a white background, a light blue border, and a bold blue font. When pressed, the button turns blue and the text turns white. These buttons are most commonly seen in the iPhone's native Address Book app.

The Buttons "Text Message" and "Add to Favorites" Are Both Rounded Rectangle Buttons

Let's say you wanted to create a button with the text "Tap Me" that changed to "I'm Being Tapped" when touched by a user. You can accomplish this with just three lines of code:

```
1  UIButton *b = [UIButton buttonWithType:UIButtonTypeRoundedRect];
2  [b setTitle:@"Tap Me!" forState:UIControlStateNormal];
3  [b setTitle:@"I'm Being Tapped" forState:UIControlStateHighlighted];
```

In line 1, we create a new UIButton using the button type UIButton-TypeRoundedRect. Next, in line 2, we set the title of the button to "Tap Me!" for the UIControlState, UIControlStateNormal. This means that under normal conditions, our button will have the title Tap Me! Finally, in line 3, we set the title text to "I'm Being Tapped" for the UIControl-State, UIControlStateHighlighted.

Notice we didn't set the UIControlStates to selected or disabled. Because we set the UIControlStateNormal value to Tap Me!, this becomes the default value for our button and will be applied to all other states if not otherwise set.

 Developer Note

To change the text properties of the button label, use the functions setTitleColor:forState: and setShadowColor:forState. In earlier versions of iOS, UIButton responded to these functions without the forState parameter. However, Apple depreciated these functions with iOS 3.0 and they should no longer be used (even if they work).

Custom Button Type

When you create a Custom button type in iOS, you are designing a button with no assumed styles. This can be very useful, especially for creating special purpose buttons such as transparent hit targets, or image overlays. Because Custom buttons start from a blank slate, setting the title without setting the background or image results in white text on a transparent background. The advantage of Custom buttons, however, is that you can now load in any image, including transparent PNGs, to create a Custom button.

Custom Buttons
Are Used to Create
Video Thumbnails

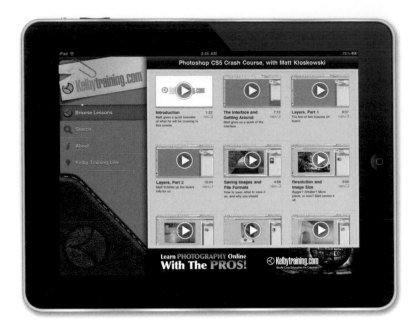

The following code block is an excellent example of when you would use a Custom UIButton button type:

```
1   //Create our thumbnail image
2   UIImage *thumbnail = [UIImage imageNamed:@"thumbnail.png"];
3   UIImageView *thumbView = [[UIImageView alloc] initWithImage:thumbnail];
4   thumbView.center = CGPointMake(180, 240);
5   [self.view addSubview:thumbView];
6
7   UIButton *b = [UIButton buttonWithType:UIButtonTypeCustom];
8   b.frame = CGRectMake(160, 220, 40, 40);
9   UIImage *play = [UIImage imageNamed:@"playbtn.png"];
10  [b setBackgroundImage:play forState:UIControlStateNormal];
11  [b addTarget:self action:@selector(playBtnPressed:)
            forControlEvents:UIControlEventTouchUpInside];
12  [self.view addSubview:b];
```

In this code block, we are setting up a thumbnail image with a Play button layered on top. Lines 2 through 5 should look familiar from Chapter 4, Basic User Interface Objects. In line 7, we go ahead and create our Custom UIButton, then define its frame in line 8. In lines 9 and 10, we set up a new UIImage that is our Play button, and set it as the background image of the UIButton. Finally in line 11, we tell our button what to do when pressed, and in line 12 we add it to our view.

You can see from this example that there are endless possibilities when setting up Custom buttons. You can turn any image into a button using the custom button type. In Chapter 12, Introduction to iOS Gestures, and Chapter 13, Creating Custom iOS Gestures, we'll discuss how to use gestures to detect touch interaction on UI elements that are not UIButtons.

Designer Note

When designing custom buttons or custom image assets, remember to keep in mind the iPhone 4's retina display. For each image asset, you should also create an image asset at two-times the resolution. Also, if an image for the selected or highlighted state is not defined in a button, iOS will automatically simulate a touch effect using a semi-transparent black layer. This means, depending on your use-case, it is not always necessary to design the touch-down state of a custom UIButton.

Get the Code ➠ ➠ ➠

Go to **fromideatoapp.com/downloads/example#buttons** to download Custom Buttons and all of the project files.

CHAPTER 8

Creating Custom UIViews and UIViewControllers

Subclassing, the inheritance of attributes, is an important part of iOS development. By this point, you should be familiar with the characteristics of a UIView that determines what the user sees, and know how the various subclasses of UIView relate to one another. You should understand the role that UIViewControllers play, and how they interact with the view life cycle.

Creating custom UIViews and UIViewControllers is a key component of designing your own iOS app. In fact, by following along with the examples in this book, you will have already created your own custom UIViewControllers—you just may not realize it.

We know that a UIViewController is used to manage an associated view and subviews, constructed either programmatically through view life cycle methods, or through the use of a nib file created in Interface Builder. By subclassing UIViewController, you can create a customized controller class with its own properties, methods, and delegates for the UI elements contained within that view.

Additionally, we know that a UIView operates as a canvas for different UI elements, defining a rectangle of specific size and location. By subclassing UIView, we can take advantage of some of the powerful Quartz 2D drawing tools that come bundled with iOS, such as blend modes, paths, transforms, and direct image and text drawing.

Custom UIViewControllers

What do we mean by custom UIViewControllers? Remember that a UIViewController defines a standard interface for interacting with its associated UIView and basic controller functions. When we create a custom UIViewController, we are starting with those baseline functions and then adding our own. These functions could be button handlers, custom delegate methods, or other user input.

From a user interface point of view, we typically use UIViewControllers to build up a custom user interface from either a *nib file* (created in Interface Builder) or manually by adding subviews in the view lifecycle methods.

Creating a New Custom UIViewController

Get the Code ➡ ➡ ➡

Go to **fromideatoapp.com/download/example#customvc** to download the completed project file and source code used in this chapter.

Create a new project in Xcode by choosing File > New Project. Just as we did in the Part I Blueprint exercise, select a Window-based iOS application. Name your project HelloInterfaceBuilder, and choose Save.

To add a custom UIViewController, simply choose File > New File from your Xcode menu.

Creating a
New File

In the New File dialog, you can choose from one of many common Cocoa Touch classes. Remember, Cocoa Touch is the UI layer on top of the core operating system and core services layer. So when we say we are creating a new Cocoa Touch class, we are creating a subclass of one of those common UI objects. For the purposes of this example, choose the UIViewController subclass and check the With XIB for user interface box. When prompted, type the name MyViewController.

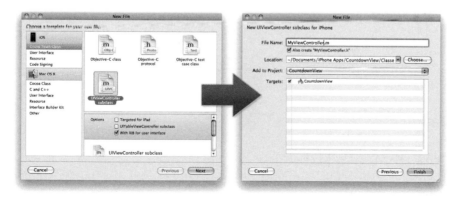

Saving
MyViewController

Tip

Explore the options in the New File dialog. You can create many different Cocoa Touch classes, including iPad optimized view controllers (which automatically rotate on orientation change) and UITableViewControllers.

Let's take a look at what Xcode created. You'll notice that Xcode added three files to your project, MyViewController.h, MyViewController.m and MyViewController.xib. These are the header file (.h), methods file (.m), and Interface Builder nib file, respectively.

In the header file, you outline various methods, properties, and protocols specific to your custom view controller; in the message file, you implement these properties and methods. The .xib Interface Builder file lets you quickly create a new UI for this UIViewController's associated view.

Looking at the header file, you should see something similar to this:

```
1   //
2   //  MyViewController.h
3   //  HelloInterfaceBuilder
4   //
5   //  Created by Shawn Welch on 12/13/10.
6   //  Copyright 2011 fromideatoapp.com All rights reserved.
7   //
8
9   #import <UIKit/UIKit.h>
10
11
12  @interface MyViewController : UIViewController {
13
14  }
15
16  @end
```

The most important line here is actually line 12. Notice the syntax, `@interface MyViewController : UIViewController`. What this line is saying is, "This header file outlines the interface for class MyView-Controller, which is a subclass of UIViewController."

If we were to change UIViewController in line 12 to another class, such as UITableViewController, MyViewController would then be a subclass of that alternate class (for example, UITableViewController). This one line defines the starting place for our custom view controller.

Note

The name MyViewController has nothing to do with the subclass itself. We could have called our class MyUIButton and still subclassed UIViewController. It is smart, however, to keep your class names consistent. When you subclass a UIView, try to include "view" in the class name. When you subclass a controller, try to include "controller" in the class name. This will help keep your code organized down the road.

Because you created your UIViewController through the New File dialog, and because you chose the UIViewController Cocoa Touch Class, Xcode automatically generated a template UIViewController subclass. You'll notice in the MyViewController.m file, Xcode has already generated some of the standard view life cycle methods for you.

Note

The goal of this book is to give you deep insight into the iOS design and development process to help you design better apps, but is not intended as a beginner's guide to Objective-C programming. Check out **fromideatoapp.com/reference#beginnersguide** for a discussion of some Objective-C basics.

Adding Properties to a Custom View Controller

Now that we have our view controller, let's add some user interface elements. Think back to some of the UI elements we've seen so far. We know that a UIButton is just a subclass of UIView, but as a button it has additional properties like a title. The title property is not part of the standard UIView class, so this must have been added in the subclass. Since we are subclassing UIViewController, we can add a title of our own to our custom view controller as well.

First, we want to add the property in our header file.

```
1   //
2   //  MyViewController.h
3   //  HelloInterfaceBuilder
4   //
5   //  Created by Shawn Welch on 12/17/10.
6   //  Copyright 2011 fromideatoapp.com All rights reserved.
7   //
8
9   #import <UIKit/UIKit.h>
10
11
12  @interface MyViewController : UIViewController {
13
14      IBOutlet UILabel *myTitle;
15
16  }
17
18  @property (nonatomic, retain) IBOutlet UILabel *myTitle;
19
20  @end
```

Here we added two lines of code, line 14 and line 18. We want to add our title, myTitle, as a property to our custom view controller. Line 14 sets up the variable in the interface of our class, while line 18 sets up the property so it can be easily set and retrieved (via getter and setter methods).

To complement line 18 in our header file, we also need to make some changes to our .m file by adding one line of code, line 12 in the following code block. Xcode uses this synthesize command to automatically generate the getter and setter methods for our UILabel, myTitle.

```
1   //
2   //  MyViewController.m
3   //  HelloInterfaceBuilder
4   //
5   //  Created by Shawn Welch on 12/17/10.
6   //  Copyright 2011 fromideatoapp.com All rights reserved.
7   //
8
9   #import "MyViewController.h"
10
11  @implementation MyViewController
12  @synthesize myTitle;
```

Note

@property and @synthesize are just convenience methods in Objective-C. When the project is built, Xcode automatically generates the necessary code to set and retrieve the values of the myTitle UILabel. This allows us to perform calls such as **myController.myTitle.text** = @"My New Text";

Once you've added line 12 to your header file, click the Build button or choose Build > Build Results in the Xcode File menu. Alternatively, you can use the keyboard shortcut, Command + Shift + B. If prompted, save all of your changes.

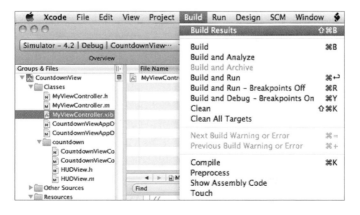

Building Your
Application

If all goes according to plan, you should see a "Succeeded" message in the bottom right corner of Xcode.

> **▶_ Developer Note**
>
> The IBOutlet identifier is simply a marker that says, Allow me to connect this property in Interface Builder. Because you identified myTitle with IBOutlet, you can directly manipulate its style and position in your view when you launch Interface Builder. If you are not using Interface Builder, you can omit IBOutlet from the code and lay out myTitle manually in the view life cycle method viewDidLoad.

Building a Custom UI Using Interface Builder

Now that you have your .m and .h files set up and successfully built in Xcode, double click MyViewController.xib in Xcode; this launches Interface Builder. Interface Builder allows you to quickly construct different user interfaces and tie them together with code written in Xcode. Because you used the IBOutlet identifier in your .h file, your .xib file automatically recognizes that this UI should have a UILabel named myTitle. All you have to do is add a label to your canvas and connect the elements to the .xib's file owner.

Interface Builder

The first thing you need to do is drag a UILabel to your view. This
automatically adds a UILabel object as a subview to the view associated with this .xib. Because this .xib was generated in combination
with your MyViewController class, Xcode has automatically associated
the view of this .xib with the view of MyViewController. Simply drag a
UILabel object from the Objects Library window onto the view canvas.

Adding a UILabel
to the Primary
View

Next, position the label where you would like your title to be, and then
select the Files Owner icon from the MyViewController.xib window.

Interface Builder
Document Window

With the Files Owner object selected, hold down the Control key and
drag your mouse over the UILabel you just added to your view.

Connecting
UILabel to File's
Owner

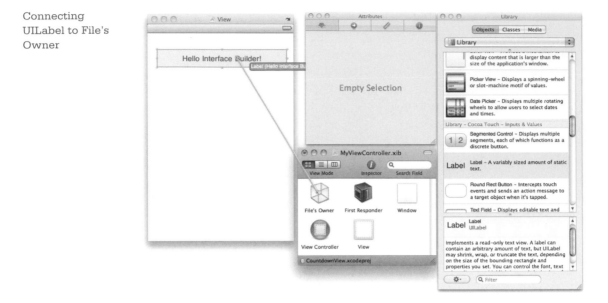

When the label is highlighted as shown, simply release your mouse and select myTitle in the small Outlets pop-up.

Tip

If you don't see myTitle in the small outlets pop-up, go back and make sure you have successfully saved and built your .m and .h files in Xcode. Interface Builder will not recognize the IBOutlet connections between itself and Xcode until the project is successfully compiled.

You're finished! You've just connected the IBOutlet you created in your .h file to the UILabel you added to the view in Interface Builder. Now you can save and quit Interface Builder.

Including and Using Custom UIViewControllers

Going back to Xcode, there is one more thing to do before you can launch your custom view controller. You'll notice that if you click the Build and Go button, your app still launches with a blank white window. You've created your custom UIViewController, but you haven't actually added the view of that view controller to the app's main window.

To do this, first select HelloInterfaceBuilderAppDelegate.m in Xcode. Near the top of this file we need to add one line of code, line 10 in the following code block:

```
1   //
2   //   HelloInterfaceBuilderAppDelegate.m
3   //   HelloInterfaceBuilder
4   //
5   //   Created by Shawn Welch on 12/13/10.
6   //   Copyright 2011 fromideatoapp.com All rights reserved.
7   //
8
9   #import "HelloInterfaceBuilderAppDelegate.h"
10  #import "MyViewController.h"
11  @implementation HelloInterfaceBuilder
12
```

By adding #import "MyViewController.h" to the top of our file, we are making our app delegate aware of the custom view controller we created. Now we can allocate our custom view controller and add its view as a subview of our main window. Without importing the header file of our custom view controller, Xcode would have thrown an error because it has no other reference to or knowledge of a class named "MyViewController."

Immediately after the applicationDidFinishLaunching method, add the following lines of code:

```
1   // allocate and initialize a new instance of MyViewController
2   // Add the view of our custom view controller as a subview of
3   // the main window. Set the text of our custom UILabel property
4   MyViewController *mvc = [[MyViewController alloc]
        initWithNibName:@"MyViewController" bundle:nil];
5   [window addSubview:mvc.view];
6   mvc.myTitle.text = @"Hello, fromideatoapp.com";
```

After adding these lines of code, build and run your app. You should now see the custom UI of your MyViewController class loaded from the .xib. Notice that because we set myTitle.text in line 6 of the code block above, the text value has changed in our UI. That is because we mapped the variable, myTitle to the IBOutlet in interface builder.

Running HelloInterface Builder in iOS Simulator

 Developer Note

We'll learn how to implement more advanced custom methods in the controller class in Chapter 9, Creating Custom Table Views and in the Part III Blueprint that follows. Chapter 9 speaks specifically to UITableViewController classes while the blueprint creates another custom UIViewController, building on our "Hello, World!" app.

Custom UIViews

Custom UIViews differ from custom UIViewControllers mainly in that UIViews focus strictly on the *view* of Model-View-Controller, while most UIViewControllers encapsulate both the view and the controller.

Custom UIViews are extremely important, however. A custom UIView is essentially a blank canvas to draw on and to use in combination with a UIViewController to create truly unique user interface. For example, in our last exercise we created a UILabel (which is a UIView subclass) and added it to our UIViewController's associated view as a subview. Depending on the needs of our user interface, we could also create a custom UIView where we draw or create a completely unique shape, and then include that custom UIView as a subview in our UIView-Controller just as we did with the UILabel. They are both, after all, subclasses of UIView.

Additionally, instead of using the auto-generated primary view of the UIViewController from Xcode, you can define the primary view of a UIViewController to be a custom UIView. After loading in your cus-tom UIView, the UIViewController will respond to view life cycle events on your custom UIView such as viewDidLoad or viewWillAppear.

The problem with creating custom UIViews is that there is no easy way to do it—certainly not as easy as using Interface Builder. To customize UIViews, you need to do most of the code by hand.

 Designer Note

It is not as important that you learn the actual code to generate the custom UIViews (trust me when I say that it will be overwhelm-ing), but rather focus your attention on learning the effects, styles, and applications of using custom UIViews. By learning what can be done through Quartz 2D drawing, you can avoid having to load unnecessary images into your app binary and ultimately save valu-able resources when your app is running.

Subclassing a UIView

Subclassing a UIView is much like subclassing any other Cocoa Touch class. You can quickly create a UIView subclass using the same New File dialog we used in the previous section. Just like the UIView-Controller, a UIView subclass needs a .h file and a .m file. Unlike a UIViewController, you cannot load a UIView using an .xib file.

After creating your UIView subclass, there are a few things to keep in mind when working with views. For now, the most important method in your .m file is drawRect. drawRect is called automatically by the iOS runtime environment every time the UIView needs to be refreshed;

this is where you will do the bulk of your drawing code. You can request that a UIView be refreshed by calling setNeedsDisplay, but as mentioned before, you should never call drawRect directly.

Because drawRect is called so frequently, you also should never allocate or manage memory from within the drawRect method. You need this method to be as fast and light as possible. Performance drops significantly if you try to allocate and create new objects from within drawRect, especially during animations. Oftentimes, it is a good idea to set up static or local variables for things like fonts and colors. These can be defined in your header or allocated when your UIView is initialized; but you should not manage these variables from within drawRect.

Also, because the goal of subclassing a UIView is to avoid creating other UI elements unnecessarily, you will rarely see other UI objects in the interface of a UIView. So, if our custom UIView draws text, we'll store the NSString value and not create a separate UILabel. If we want to draw an image, we'll use UIImage, and not a UIImageView. We will be drawing these data types directly on the canvas, so we don't want the extra weight of a UIView wrapper like UILabel or UIImageView—our subclass is its own wrapper optimized for our needs.

Finally, instead of just letting the Xcode compiler synthesize our setter methods like we did with HelloInterfaceBuilder, we'll override the setter so that when our custom UIView receives a new data value, we can call [self setNeedsDisplay] to refresh the new data in our UIView.

Quartz 2D and the Graphics Context

Quartz 2D made its debut with Mac OS X as a part of Core Graphics framework. Because iOS is based on Mac OS X, your iOS apps can take advantage of the exact same 2D drawing, animation, and rendering technology available in full Mac OS X computers.

Quartz 2D is extremely powerful, and warrants an entire book just to itself. You can use it to render custom shapes, graphics, gradients, and shadows, or even create dynamic PDF documents. In the interest of time, however, we will focus on one of the most common tasks. This section will walk you through how to directly draw in the graphics context of a subclassed UIView.

The graphics context is the destination of your Quartz 2D drawing. It contains all of the device information, paths, colors, line thickness, and so on. When you subclass UIView and override the drawRect method, start by getting a reference to the graphics context for that view.

```
1   CGContextRef context = UIGraphicsGetCurrentContext();
```

Throughout the drawRect method, you'll use this graphics context as the destination of any drawing, painting, paths, transforms, or shadows. There are four key components of Quartz 2D drawing you need to know to master subclassing UIViews and overriding drawRect:

- Paths
- Transforms
- Images and blend modes
- Text

> **Developer Note**
>
> Quartz 2D can do a lot more than is explained in this chapter. Check out **fromideatoapp.com/reference#quartz2d** for more advanced lessons and tutorials.

Paths

Paths can be extremely useful for creating custom shapes. A path works exactly like it sounds. If you think of your UIView as a canvas, drawing a path means moving between two points on that canvas and stroking or filling the resulting shape at the end. You are not limited to moving along a straight line. In fact, you can traverse your canvas using points, lines, arcs, cubic Bézier curves, quadratic Bézier curves, ellipses, and rectangles. The following code example creates a simple 200 x 200 square filled with 66 percent black.

```
1   CGFloat height = 200; // Set Height Constant
2   CGFloat width = 200;  // Set Width Constant
3
4   // Get Graphics Context
```

continues

```
5   CGContextRef context = UIGraphicsGetCurrentContext();
6
7   // Set fill color to 66% black
8   CGContextSetRGBFillColor(context, 0, 0, 0, .66);
9
10  // Move path to origin (0,0)
11  CGContextMoveToPoint(context, 0, 0);
12
13  // Move path to (width,0)
14  CGContextAddLineToPoint(context, width, 0);
15
16  // Move path to (width,height)
17  CGContextAddLineToPoint(context, width, height);
18
19  // Move path to (0,height)
20  CGContextAddLineToPoint(context, 0, height);
21
22  // Move path to origin (0,0)
23  CGContextAddLineToPoint(context, 0, 0);
24
25  // Fill path with fill color
26  CGContextFillPath(context);
```

Transforms

Transform functions allow you to rotate, scale, or translate your graphics context. In Chapter 11, Creating Custom iOS Animations, we'll discuss how to animate the transforms of a UIView.

```
1   CGContextTranslateCTM(context, 100, 50);        //Translate orig (100,50)
2   CGContextRotateCTM(context, radians(-85));      //Rotate context -85 degrees
3   CGContextScaleCTM(context, .5, .5);             //Scale context by 50%
```

Images and Blend Modes

Remember that a UIImage is simply the data type that stores necessary image data. When we first discussed UIImages and UIImageViews, we had to use a UIImageView so we could add an image as a subview to an existing view. Here, because we're drawing directly onto a graphics context, all we need is the image data itself.

There are a few different methods for drawing images onto a graphics context. Each method is self-explanatory; essentially you can either draw an image from an origin point, or within a CGRect using an alpha or blend mode component:

- drawAtPoint:(CGPoint)point;

- drawAtPoint:(CGPoint)point blendMode:(CGBlendMode)blendMode alpha:(CGFloat)alpha;

- drawInRect:(CGRect)rect;

- drawInRect:(CGRect)rect blendMode:(CGBlendMode)blendMode alpha:(CGFloat)alpha;

- drawAsPatternInRect:(CGRect)rect;

```
1  UIImage *flower = [UIImage imageNamed:@"flower.png"]; //Create UIImage
2  [flower drawInRect:CGRectMake(0, 0, 320, 240);  //draw in 320x240 rect
```

Constant	Blend Mode
kCGBlendModeNormal	Normal
kCGBlendModeMultiply	Multiply
kCGBlendModeScreen	Screen
kCGBlendModeOverlay	Overlay
kCGBlendModeDarken	Darken
kCGBlendModeLighten	Lighten
kCGBlendModeColorDodge	Color Dodge
kCGBlendModeColorBurn	Color Burn
kCGBlendModeSoftLight	Soft Light
kCGBlendModeHardLight	Hard Light
kCGBlendModeDifference	Difference
kCGBlendModeExclusion	Exclusion

TABLE 8.1 Graphics Context Blend Modes

continues

TABLE 8.1
continued

Constant	Blend Mode
kCGBlendModeHue	Hue
kCGBlendModeSaturation	Saturation
kCGBlendModeColor	Color
kCGBlendModeLuminosity	Luminosity

Text

Finally, we can draw NSStrings directly using the drawInRect methods
available. As with UIImages, we can draw text in a rectangle or in
a specific point. The following code samples assume we have created a
local font variable of type UIFont named sys.

```
1   //Draw in Rect with Font
2   [@"iOS apps" drawInRect:CGRectMake(0, 0, 320, 30)
                withFont:sys];
3
4   //Draw in Rect with Font and Line Break Mode
5   [@"iOS apps" drawInRect:CGRectMake(0, 0, 320, 30)
                withFont:sys
          lineBreakMode:UILineBreakModeTailTruncation];
6
7   //Draw in Rect with Font, Line Break Mode, and alignment
8   [@"iOS apps" drawInRect:CGRectMake(0, 0, 320, 30)
                withFont:sys
          lineBreakMode:UILineBreakModeMiddleTruncation
              alignment:UITextAlignmentLeft];
```

Get the Code ➡ ➡ ➡

Go to **fromideatoapp.com/downloads/example#quartz2d** to download
Quartz2D and all of the project files including some that were not discussed in this chapter.

CHAPTER 9

Creating Custom Table Views

One of the most common UIViewController subclasses you'll use in your apps is the UITableViewController—used to display and manage information in a table view. The UITableViewController is so important that I've dedicated this entire chapter to teaching you how to customize this one class. Table views are designed to communicate long lists of information to users effectively and efficiently. When you look at the Mail app, Apple uses a table view to present the list of emails in your inbox. Also, when you look at the Settings app, a cell in a table view represents each preference or setting.

Table views are diverse. You can customize their appearance to look like anything from the SMS app to the Contacts app—but in terms of underlying structure, both of these apps use a table view subclass to present long scrolling lists of information. It is easy to make mistakes when creating table views. If you're not paying attention, you'll create a table that's jerky and slow to respond. To avoid these pitfalls, we'll learn how table views work, and discuss various methods for creating and manipulating them.

UITableViewController

The UITableViewController is a subclass of UIViewController (i.e., controller methods, view life cycle methods, etc.) where the associated view is a UITableView. As you recall, UITableView is a subclass of the UIScrollView thus giving it the ability to scroll. In addition to the methods declared in the interface of the UIViewController, the UITableViewController defines methods for controlling the data and the appearance of its associated table view. A UITableView must have a data source and a delegate. By default, a UITableViewController is configured to serve as both the data source and delegate for its associated table view. It sounds a bit complicated, so let's first visit what the table view controller's delegate and data source actually do for our table view.

How a Table View Works

When trying to visualize how the UITableView works, it's best to remember the Model-View-Controller paradigm. Remember the view (the UITableView) is completely separate from the model and controller. This means, that the UITableView is helpless without a delegate and data source. Fortunately, the UITableViewController will automatically assign itself as both data source and delegate when one is not previously defined.

To configure the appearance, data, and behavior of the table view in your UITableViewController, you need to implement the methods found in the UITableViewDataSource and UITableViewDelegate protocols.

UITableView Data Source

The data source of a UITableView provides the information needed to display and modify information on the screen. When the UITableView is first loaded on the screen, it asks its data source a series of questions: How many rows are in this table? How many sections? What is the title of section 1? What does the cell look like in section 1, row 3? and so on. Of course, they're not phrased as actual questions.

Instead, the data source conforms to a protocol called the *UITableViewDataSource* protocol. The data source will implement the methods defined in the UITableViewDataSource protocol (see Table 9.1), and the UITableView will call those methods when it needs the information.

Method	Description
`tableView:cellForRowAtIndexPath:` *	Return the UITableViewCell object for a given row and section
`numberOfSectionsInTableView:`	Return the number of **sections** in the table view
`tableView:numberOfRowsInSection:` *	Return the number of **rows** in a specific section of the table view
`sectionIndexTitlesForTableView:`	Return an array of titles to be used in the right side "quick scroll", traditionally letters A to Z
`tableView:sectionForSectionIndexTitle: atIndex:`	Return the index of the section mapped to the index of the sidebar titles
`tableView:titleForHeaderInSection:`	Return the title for a specific section
`tableView:titleForFooterInSection:`	Return the footer string for a specific section

TABLE 9.1
UITableView-
DataSource
Protocol

*required

UITableView Delegate

Much like the data source, the delegate responds to a series of questions asked by the table view and conforms to the protocol UITableViewDelegate. Unlike the data source, however, instead of responding to questions about the content, the delegate also responds to actions taken on the table view, such as "User selected row 1 in section 3." It is the delegate's responsibility to take that action and decide what to do as a result. (The UITableViewDelegate Protocol is described in Table 9.2.)

Method	Description
`tableView:heightForRowAtIndexPath:`	Return the height for a specific row
`tableView:indentationLevelForRowAt`➡`IndexPath:`	Return the indentation level of a specific row
`tableView:willDisplayCell: forRowAtIndexPath:`	Notification that a cell will soon be displayed, similar to view life cycle method, viewWillAppear:
`tableView:accessoryButtonTappedForRow`➡`WithIndexPath:`	Notification that a user selected an accessory button on a given row
`tableView:willSelectRowAtIndexPath:`	Notification that a user will select a row
`tableView:didSelectRowAtIndexPath:`	Notification that a user did select a row
`tableView:willDeselectRowAtIndexPath:`	Notification that a user will deselect a row
`tableView:didDeselectRowAtIndexPath:`	Notification that a user did deselect row

TABLE 9.2
UITableView-
Delegate Protocol

continues

TABLE 9.2
continued

Method	Description
`tableView:viewForHeaderInSection:`	Return a custom UIView to be used as the header in a specific section
`tableView:viewForFooterInSection:`	Return a custom UIView to be used as the footer in a specific section
`tableView:heightForHeaderInSection:`	Return the height for the header in a specific section
`tableView:heightForFooterInSection:`	Return the height for the footer in a specific section
`tableView:willBeginEditingRowAtIndexPath:`	Notification that editing will begin soon at a specific row
`tableView:didEndEditingRowAtIndexPath:`	Notification that editing has ended at a specific row
`tableView:editingStyleForRowAtIndexPath:`	Return the possible editing styles for a specific row; options include Delete, Insert, or none
`tableView:titleForDeleteConfirmationButtonFor➡RowAtIndexPath:`	Return a string to be used as the title in the red delete confirmation, e.g., the Mail app replaces delete with "Archive" in some exchange servers
`tableView:shouldIndentWhileEditingRowAtIndexPath:`	Return a Boolean determining if indentation is allowed while editing a specific row

UITableView Appearance

Not all of the properties of the table view are controlled by the delegate and data source protocols. The table view itself has a set of properties that directly impact its appearance and behavior, most notably, the UITableViewStyle.

UITableViewStyle

When you first initialize your UITableView, you must choose between one of two UITableViewStyles: plain (UITableViewStylePlain) or grouped (UITableViewStyleGrouped). The plain table view style is, as you might expect, square rows on a white background. The most common example of a plain table view is the inbox in the native Mail app or Contacts app. The grouped table view style, however, creates white cells with rounded corners grouped together in sections on a special gray-striped background. The best example of a grouped table view can be found in the native Settings app on the iPhone or iPod touch.

Examples of
UITableViewStyle-
Plain (left) and
UITableViewStyle-
Grouped (right)

Tip

The background color of the UITableViewStyleGrouped is a system color
called groupTableViewBackgroundColor. Use [UIColor groupTableView-
BackgroundColor]; to create this patterned color outside the grouped
table view style.

UITableViewCell

Recall from Chapter 4, Basic User Interface Objects, that each row in
the table view is actually a subview called a UITableViewCell. When a
table view is shown on the screen, iOS allocates enough cells in memory
to display the necessary information on the screen.

As the user scrolls down and cells are pushed off the screen, they are
moved around and repositioned so they can be reused to display cells
just starting to come onto the screen. This allows the table view to be
extremely memory efficient by only allocating enough memory for the
cells currently visible on the screen. A table view with 10,000 cells will
perform just as well as a table view with only 10.

When the table view needs to display a new row, it calls the method
tableView:cellForRowAtIndexPath: on its data source. In this method
you can check to see if there is a cell available for reuse, or allocate a
new cell in memory. We'll cover the actual code of this method in the
blueprint following this chapter.

Table View Cell Styles

You can also take advantage of one of the many UITableViewCellStyles. Each cell is configured to give you a unique look while needing to set only a handful of properties, such as textLabel, detailTextLabel, imageView, and accessoryType. These properties are, of course, optional; you are not required to use any of them when creating your cells.

- UITableViewCellStyleDefault: Left-aligned, bold text label with optional image view.

- UITableViewCellStyleValue1: Left-aligned text label with right-aligned, blue text label (used in the native Settings app).

- UITableViewCellStyleValue2: Right-aligned, blue text label on the left with left-aligned text label on the right (used in the native Address Book app for contact details). Unlike the other styles, this one does not have an image view. Below illustrates two cell styles in a grouped table using this style.

- UITableViewCellStyleSubtitle: Left-aligned label on top with left-aligned, lighter gray label underneath (used in the native Mail app).

Note

In addition to these properties, each cell has a contentView property. The contentView is simply an empty UIView that is positioned on the cell. We'll use the contentView later on when we create our own custom cell layouts.

Table View Cell Accessory View

The accessory view provides decoration or functionality on the right edge of the cell. You can choose from one of four accessory types:

- UITableViewCellAccessoryNone

- UITableViewCellAccessoryDisclosureIndicator

- UITableViewCellAccessoryDetailDisclosureButton

- UITableViewCellAccessoryCheckmark

In addition to these accessory view styles, you have the option to set a custom UIView as the UITableViewCellAccessoryView. For example, it is common to use a UISwitch as the UITableViewCellAccessoryView, giving users the option to toggle preferences on and off.

Custom Table View Cell Accessory View

Developer Note

It is very important to reuse cells whenever possible and to avoid allocating new cells in memory. Your app will very quickly become unusable, slow to respond, and jerky if you do not reuse cells. When you reuse cells, reconfigure each cell for the current row. For example, if your new row does not have a detailTextLabel or image, but the cell you are reusing did, make sure you clear out that data. Because the cell is being reused, all of its data is still intact from the last time it was used. If you fail to clear it out, the data will be displayed on the screen when the cell is reused. Check out the Table View Programming Guide for iOS at **fromideatoapp.com/ reference#tableview** for more information on Table Views.

Table Header and Footer View

Each table view has a UIView associated with the header and footer. By default, these views are set to nil. You can create a custom UIView and then set it as the header or footer view. In the following code block, lines 1 through 5 simply create a new UILabel. In line 6, we set that label as our tableHeaderView. Similarly, in lines 8 through 12 we create a second UILabel, which is then set as our tableFooterView in line 13.

```
1   UILabel *hd = [[UILabel alloc] initWithFrame:CGRectMake(0, 0, 320,50)];
2   hd.backgroundColor = [UIColor blackColor];
3   hd.textColor = [UIColor whiteColor];
4   hd.textAlignment = UITextAlignmentCenter;
5   hd.text = @"Header";
6   [tableView setTableHeaderView:hd];
7
8   UILabel *ft = [[UILabel alloc] initWithFrame:CGRectMake(0, 0, 320,50)];
9   ft.backgroundColor = [UIColor blackColor];
10  ft.textColor = [UIColor whiteColor];
11  ft.textAlignment = UITextAlignmentCenter;
12  ft.text = @"Footer";
13  [tableView setTableFooterView:ft];
```

Creating Custom Cells

In previous chapters, we learned two ways of creating UIViews that are unique to our UI. The first technique involved adding a series of subviews to a parent view, and the second involved subclassing UIView and drawing directly in the view's graphics context. Creating custom table view cells is just as simple—which makes sense, since we know the UITableViewCell is just a subclass of UIView. You can use custom table view cells to provide additional application specific information not possible with the default table view cell styles.

There are two primary techniques for creating custom cells. Just like with our standard UIView subclass, we can either:

- Subclass UITableViewCell and build a custom view hierarchy on each cell.
- Override the drawRect function of our table view cell's contentView and draw on the graphics context directly.

Picture, for example, the iPod app's table view cell. In the left you have a UIImage for the cover art, and in the center you have a UILabel for the song title. All of these objects rest as a subview to the cell's view. In addition to those UI elements, iOS creates an additional blank layer that you can use to create custom views. Because this blank layer, or contentView, covers our cell, we can either add subviews or override the drawRect function

```
1   [self.contentView addSubview:myCustomTextLabel];
```

In this code sample, self represents our subclassed UITableViewCell, while myCustomTextLabel is a UILabel that we have created separately.

Pros and Cons

Each technique provides its own list of pros and cons. When building a custom view hierarchy for each cell, you are able to leverage the simplicity of existing iOS elements such as labels and image views by adding them as subviews to the contentView. The disadvantage of this method is that as your cells get more and more complicated, iOS can get bogged down with needing to retain in memory a complicated view hierarchy for each cell.

On the other side of the equation, by overriding the drawRect function of our contentView, we decrease the number of objects iOS has to retain (thus decreasing the complexity of our contentView's view hierarchy) by drawing directly on the cell. But drawing on the contentView directly means we have to recreate the functionality of standard iOS elements such as labels and image views ourselves.

For more information and detailed code samples on how to create custom table view cell subclasses as well as examples for overriding the contentView's drawRect method, please refer to the Part III Blueprint, Custom iOS UI.

Designer Note

When designing your UI or creating your user experiences, try to anticipate whether or not your developer will be able to use a default cell style, or whether they will need to create a custom UITableViewCell. Remember when a user scrolls on a table view, iOS will reuse cells to display information. Be mindful of what elements are consistent in each cell and what elements are unique. For example ask yourself, will iOS be able to reuse the same text label or image view as a user scrolls?

Moving, Deleting, and Inserting Rows

You may have noticed that the data source and delegate methods referenced moving, inserting, and deleting rows. The APIs in the iOS SDK make it very easy to manage the content of your table views dynamically. To make a table view editable, however, you must implement a few methods in your table view data source and delegate. To help visualize what methods are needed, let's walk through what happens when a user taps an Edit button located in the top UINavigationBar. We'll start with reordering (moving) rows.

> **Developer Note**
>
> These examples will walk you through the process of moving, deleting, and inserting rows in a UITableView. For code examples, please refer to the Part III blueprint that follows this chapter, or visit **fromideatoapp.com/downloads/example#tableview**, where you can download all project files for the examples in this chapter.

Reordering Rows in a Table View

Below are the steps invoked between a table view and its delegate and data source while reordering rows in a UITableView.

1. User taps Edit button. Button handler in our **controller** calls `setEditing:animated:` on the table view.

2. Table calls `tableView:canMoveRowAtIndexPath:` in our **delegate** for all visible rows (and any rows that become visible if the user scrolls while in editing mode). This returns a Boolean value indicating whether or not a particular row can be moved.

    At this point, our table view is in edit mode. All rows that returned YES, indicating they can be moved, are identified with a reorder control located on the right edge of the table view cell (see the figure on the following page).

3. User drags a row that is eligible for reordering. Our table view calls `tableView:targetIndexPathForMoveFromRowAtIndexPath:toProposedIndexPath:` on our **delegate**, essentially asking if the proposed destination is allowed.

4. User drops the row in a new (approved) location. Our table view calls `tableView:moveRowAtIndexPath:toIndexPath:` on our **data source**. The data source updates the data-model, reorganizing any information to reflect the new row positions.

> **Designer Note**
>
> Reorder controls are a standard element in the iOS SDK. You cannot change the appearance of these without completely recreating the UITableView from scratch. If your app calls for the ability to reorder table views, it is recommended that you use the standard controls.

Reordering and
Deleting Rows in a
UITableView

User drags to move row   User taps to delete row

Get the Code ⟫ ⟫ ⟫

Go to **fromideatoapp.com/downloads/example#tableview** to download
TableViews and all of the project files.

Inserting and Deleting Rows

Here are the steps invoked between a table view and its delegate and
data source while inserting or deleting rows in a UITableView.

1. User taps the Edit button. The button handler in our **controller**
   calls `setEditing:animated:` on the table view.

2. Table view calls `tableView:canEditRowAtIndexPath:` in our **data
   source** for all visible rows (and any rows that become visible if the
   user scrolls while in editing mode).

3. Table view calls `tableView:editingStyleForRowAtIndexPath:` in our
   delegate for all rows that returned YES in step 2.

   After step 3, our table view is in editing mode. Rows that were identified by the delegate to be deleted in step 3 have a red minus button
   next to them, while rows that were identified to be inserted have a
   green plus button next to them.

4. User taps the minus button and a red Delete button animates in from the right side of the cell. Our table view calls
   `tableView:titleForDeleteConfirmationButtonForRowAtIndexPath`

on our **delegate** (if implemented) for an alternate title on the Delete button. If this method is not implemented, the button just reads "delete" (see figure on previous page).

5. User taps the Delete button. Our table view calls `tableView:commit EditingStyle:forRowAtIndexPath:` on the **data source** where the data source is expected to update the data-model and remove the necessary row information. Additionally, this method should call `deleteRowsAtIndexPaths:withRowAnimation:` or `insertRowsAtInd cxPaths:withRowAnimation:` on our table view to remove the actual row from our view.

> **Developer Note**
>
> This series of events outlines what occurs when a user taps an Edit button and invokes the setEditing method on our entire table view. Similarly, if you don't want an Edit button but include `canEditRowAtIndexPath` and `commitEditingStyle:forRowAt IndexPath:` in your data source and delegate, respectively, iOS automatically implements the "swipe to delete" function. When the user swipes a row, the table view follows similar steps, but only invokes calls relative to the individual cell that was swiped.

As you can see from these workflows, it's easy to rearrange, insert, or delete rows in a table view as long as you're aware of the tight relation ship between the table view, the delegate, and the data source. These examples also highlight the importance of the Model-View-Controller relationship in iOS development. You can clearly see which methods control the model (data source), which methods control the controller (delegate), and which methods control the view (table view).

Custom iOS UI

In Part III, Designing Custom iOS User Interface Objects, we learned how to create custom UI elements and how to subclass various view controllers. Before you begin this blueprint, you'll need some additional assets. Go to **fromideatoapp.com/downloads/bp3_assets.zip** to download the image files and fast-draw table view subclass.

Get the Code ⫸ ⫸ ⫸

This blueprint involves a lot of code and the creation of files. If you get lost, or feel more comfortable following along with a completed project, go to **fromideatoapp.com/downloads/blueprints** to download FI2ADemo.

Overview

In general, we'll be working with the same project we created in the Part II blueprint. To give us some direction, we'll replace the UIView-Controllers we used as tabs with subclasses of UITableViewController and wrap them in a UINavigationController before placing them in our UITabBarController. The first tab will be a custom UITableView-Controller with a custom UITabBarItem. The second tab will use our fast-draw table view cell technique. Unfortunately, in the interest of space, the second portion of this blueprint will be continued online at **fromideatoapp.com/downloads/blueprints**, project FI2ADemo.

Changes to the First Tab

In our first tab, we'll create a simple table view using the grouped style, but customize it with a custom tab bar item. Additionally, we'll move the UI elements and controller methods from our app delegate (created in the previous blueprint) into a new UIViewController subclass called DetailViewController. When a user taps a row in our table view controller, the detail view controller will be animated onto the navigation stack.

To make these modifications, we'll perform the following steps:

1. Create new files in Xcode (allow Xcode to generate templates).

2. Add downloaded image assets nav_home.png and nav_home@2x.png to app resources.

3. Move UI elements and control methods from the app delegate (created in the previous blueprint) to the detail view controller.

4. Move the tab bar set up from the app delegate (created in the previous blueprint) to the initialization of the new view controller.

5. Implement the table view data source and delegate methods to control row appearance and the didSelectRowAtIndexPath function.

Step 1

The first thing we need to do is create header and method files for our custom subclasses. For the UITableViewController, choose *File > New File* to open a new file. With Cocoa Touch Class selected in the left navigation pane, choose UIViewController and **check the box** labeled: *UITableViewController subclass*. Select Next and name the file T1_TableViewController. Then repeat these steps, but this time choose UIViewController and **uncheck the box** labeled: *UIViewController subclass*. Select Next and save the file as DetailViewController.

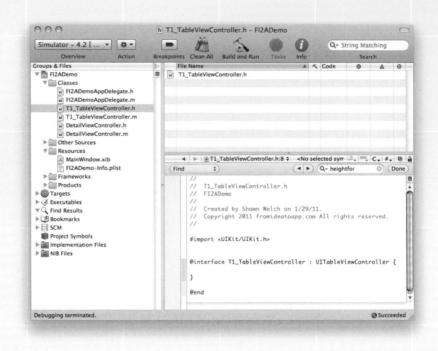

Step 2

Next, drag the image assets nav_home.png and nav_home@2x.png into the project's resource folder. This will make the image assets available for use in the custom tab bar item.

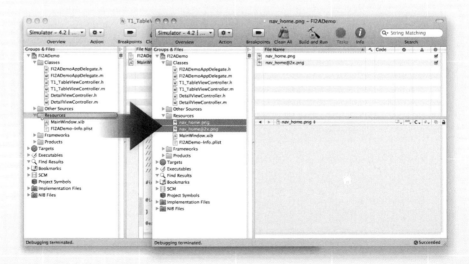

Step 3

Next, move the UI elements and controller methods from the app delegate into the .m and .h files of the DetailViewController. Remember, when a user selects a row in the T1_TableViewController, we'll allocate a new DetailViewController and push it onto the stack.

DetailViewController.h

```
1   #import <UIKit/UIKit.h>
2
3   @interface DetailViewController : UIViewController {
4
5       UILabel *label1;
6       UITextField *input;
7
8   }
9
10  - (void)changeText:(id)sender;
11
12  @end
```

DetailViewController.m

```
1   // Implement viewDidLoad to do additional setup
2   // after loading the view, typically from a nib.
3   - (void)viewDidLoad {
4       [super viewDidLoad];
5
6       self.view.backgroundColor = [UIColor groupTableViewBackgroundColor];
7
8       // Create a UITextField Input with frame (x,y,width,height)
9       // Set text field border style to Rounded Rect
10      // Add our text field to tab1's view
11      input = [[UITextField alloc]
             initWithFrame:CGRectMake(20, 20, 280, 30)];
```

```
12      input.borderStyle = UITextBorderStyleRoundedRect;
13      [self.view addSubview:input];
14
15      // Create a button with type Rounded Rect
16      // Set the frame of our button (x,y,width,height)
17      // Set the text of our button for control state normal
18      // Add our button to this view controller's view (tab 1)
19      UIButton *button = [UIButton buttonWithType:UIButtonTypeRoundedRect];
20      button.frame = CGRectMake(20, 70, 280, 40);
21      [button setTitle:@"Set Text" forState:UIControlStateNormal];
22      [self.view addSubview:button];
23
24      // Create a label with frame (x,y,width,height)
25      // Set the text alignment of our label to "center"
26      // Add our label to this view controller's view (tab 1)
27      label1 = [[UILabel alloc]
              initWithFrame:CGRectMake(20, 120, 280, 40)];
28      label1.textAlignment = UITextAlignmentCenter;
29      label1.backgroundColor = [UIColor clearColor];
30      label1.textColor = [UIColor darkGrayColor];
31      label1.shadowColor = [UIColor whiteColor];
32      label1.shadowOffset = CGSizeMake(0, 1);
33      label1.text = @"Tap \"Set Text\" to Change Me";
34      label1.font = [UIFont systemFontOfSize:14];
35      [self.view addSubview:label1];
36
37      // Add an action to our button
38      //  - Set the target to self, this is where
39      //     we implement the action
40      //  - Set the action to call method changeText:
41      //  - Call the action for event "touch up inside"
```

```
42       //     (call when the finger lifts up on the button)
43       [button addTarget:self
                     action:@selector(changeText:)
               forControlEvents:UIControlEventTouchUpInside];
44  }
45
46  - (void)changeText:(id)sender{
47       label1.text = input.text;
48       [input endEditing:YES];
49  }
```

There's a lot of code in this section, but let's see if we can parse out exactly what we've done. The first block of code, DetailViewController.h, mirrors what we did in the previous blueprint. We're simply setting up instance variables to be accessed from the controller at some other time.

Notice how the second block of code, DetailViewController.m, is in the viewDidLoad method. Remember our discussion about the view life cycle. The viewDidLoad method will be called on our view controller right after its associated view has been loaded into memory. In lines 3 through 44, we follow the same basic principles we did in the previous blueprint. The only difference (besides a few cosmetic enhancements) is that we call addSubview on self.view, instead of tab1.view. Remember, "self" refers to the current class you're working in. So what we're saying in these lines of code is (speaking as our custom UIViewController), "add the view as a subview of my associated view."

Step 4

For this step, we'll be working in the T1_TableViewController.m file. In the previous blueprint, we created a UITabBarItem using a system tab bar style. Here we'll move the UITabBarItem set up from the app delegate to the initialization of the T1_TableViewController, and set up a custom tab bar item instead of using a system-provided tab bar item.

If you open your T1_TableViewController.m file, you'll notice near the top there is a method named initWithStyle that is colored green. Green means this method is commented out (so iOS will ignore it).

Remove the /* and */ before and after the method to uncomment the code block. Next, copy the UITabBarItem set up from the app delegate into this method. This time, instead of setting up tab bar item using initWithTabBarSystemItem, use initWithTitle:image:tag.

```
1   - (id)initWithStyle:(UITableViewStyle)style {
2       // Override initWithStyle: if you create the controller
3       // programmatically and want to perform customization that
4       // is not appropriate for viewDidLoad.
5       self = [super initWithStyle:style];
6           if (self) {
7               // Set the title, this will be shown
8               //   if a UINavigationController
9               //   is our parent view controller
10              self.title = @"FI2ADemo: Tab 1";
11
12              // Create a new tab bar item (UITabBarController icon)
13              //     using a custom title and UIImage
14              // Set the new tab bar item as the TabBarItem for self
15              // Clean up memory, we don't need tbi1 anymore
16              UITabBarItem *tbi1 = [[UITabBarItem alloc]
                    initWithTitle:@"Home"
                    image:[UIImage imageNamed:@"nav_home.png"]
                    tag:0];
17              [self setTabBarItem:tbi1];
18              [tbi1 release];
19          }
20      return self;
21  }
```

In line 17, instead of calling **setTabBarItem** on tab1 as we did in the previous blueprint, we call **setTabBarItem** on self, to set the tab bar for this UITableViewController subclass.

Step 5

Finally, we need to implement the UITableView data source and delegate methods:

- numberOfSectionsInRow
- numberOfRowsInSection
- cellForRowAtIndexPath
- didSelectRowAtIndexPath

The first three methods are defined in the UITableView data source protocol. The last method, didSelectRowAtIndexPath, is defined in the UITableView delegate protocol. Remember, by default, the data source and delegate of UITableViewController are set to self.

```
1   - (NSInteger)numberOfSectionsInTableView:(UITableView *)tableView {
2       // Return the number of sections.
3       return 1;
4   }
5
6   - (NSInteger)tableView:(UITableView *)tableView
    numberOfRowsInSection:(NSInteger)section {
7       // Return the number of rows in the section.
8       return 10;
9   }
10
11  // Customize the appearance of table view cells.
12  - (UITableViewCell *)tableView:(UITableView *)tableView
            cellForRowAtIndexPath:(NSIndexPath *)indexPath {
13
14      static NSString *CellIdentifier = @"Cell";
15      // Find a cell to reuse, if you can't make a new one
16      UITableViewCell *cell = [tableView
            dequeueReusableCellWithIdentifier:CellIdentifier];
17      if (cell == nil) {
```

```
18            cell = [[[UITableViewCell alloc]
                    initWithStyle:UITableViewCellStyleDefault
                        reuseIdentifier:CellIdentifier] autorelease];
19        }
20
21        // Set the row number as the text string in our cell
22        cell.textLabel.text = [NSString
            stringWithFormat:@"Row %d",indexPath.row];
23        return cell;
24  }
25
26  - (void)tableView:(UITableView *)tableView
            didSelectRowAtIndexPath:(NSIndexPath *)indexPath {
27        // Create detail view controller, push on to navigation stack
28        DetailViewController *detail = [[DetailViewController alloc]
            initWithNibName:nil bundle:nil];
29        detail.title = [NSString stringWithFormat:@"Row %d",indexPath.row];
30        [self.navigationController pushViewController:detail animated:YES];
31        [detail release];
32  }
```

Note

Remember to import DetailViewController.h at the top of your
T1_TableViewController.m file. By importing it, we tell the custom
UITableViewController that DetailViewController exists.

Get the Code ➠ ➠ ➠

In the interest of space, we had to cut this blueprint short and continue
it online. To continue this tutorial and download the entire project, go to
fromideatoapp.com/downloads/blueprints and select FI2ADemo.

PART IV

Animating Your UI

CHAPTER 10

Introduction to iOS Animations

Everybody loves animations. In fact, Apple uses animations throughout iOS that go almost unnoticed—from the subtle disappearance of toolbars and status bars, to the iconic genie effect used on email messages when they are deleted. In Chapter 8, Creating Custom UIViews and UIViewControllers, we talked a little bit about Core Graphics, an Objective-C framework that gives you direct access to the 2D drawing capabilities of Quartz 2D. The animation counterpart to Core Graphics is Core Animation. Leveraging a similar Objective-C framework, Core Animation is a high-performance compositing engine that lets you create your own complex animations in iOS apps.

But let's take a step back, because this is just an introduction to iOS animations. In Chapter 11, Creating Custom iOS Animations, we'll talk about how we can leverage the power of Core Animations. For now, however, we'll talk about the animation capabilities built into UIKit.

About Animations Using UIKit

Early on we learned that UIKit outlines the fundamental framework for dealing with user interface elements. From UIKit we get app windows, views, controls, and more; UIKit has everything we need for a touch-based user interface. In addition to these UI elements, however, UIKit has a simple API for animating and transitioning views. The same Core Animation frameworks we will use to create animations power these high-level methods. Because it is built into UIKit, however, a lot of the more complicated low-level programming is already taken care of.

While you don't have as much control as you would with direct access to Core Animation, you'll find that animating UIViews through the UIKit API can be simple and effective.

This is an important distinction between the UIKit animation API and Core Animation. The UIKit API allows us to animate UI elements that are descendants of UIView. Essentially, we'll be animating those classes that are already wrapped inside UIKit. As in Chapter 8, when we started creating our own views, once we step outside the UIKit framework and begin manipulating the Graphics Context directly within drawRect, we'll be unable to use the UIKit animation API. If we want to design animations to manipulate the properties available only in the drawRect method, we'll need to use Core Animation.

Until then, however, the UIKit animation API will work extremely well for animating UI elements from our UIViewController view life cycle methods, because these methods typically deal with a hierarchy of UIView subviews.

What Properties Can Be Animated?

The methods in the UIKit animation API are actually defined in the interface of our base UIView class. This means two things:

- Any of the UI elements that are subclasses of UIView can be animated.
- All of the properties that you can animate must be defined in the base UIView class.

Naturally, since we know that a UIView defines a basic rectangle of specific size and location, it's reasonable to assume that we can animate these properties. In fact we can, along with a few other basic properties you'll find in the UIView. As discussed in Chapter 4, Basic User Interface Objects, the UIView defines an object with a frame, bounds, center, transform, opacity, backgroundColor, and contentStretch. All of these properties can be animated using the animation APIs found in UIView (see Table 10.1).

Property	Description
frame	The frame of a view defines the height and width of the rectangle with the origin as the origin location in the view's superview
bounds	The bounds of a view also define the same height and width, but the origin is with respect to the current view, and is usually (0,0)
center	The center defines the view's position in its superview
transform	The transformation of a view defines the scale, rotation, or translation of a view relative to its center point. The UIKit API limits transformations to a 2D space (3D transformations must be done using Core Animation)
alpha	The overall opacity of the view
backgroundColor	The background color of the view
contentStretch	The mode by which the contents of a view are stretched to fill the available space. For example, an image within a UIImageView that is scale-to-fill might be animated to scale-to-fit

TABLE 10.1
Properties of UIView that Can Be Animated

UIView Animation Blocks

When you animate views using the UIKit API, you actually create a series of UIView animation blocks. These blocks are self-contained animations that can be nested or strung together into a series. You can assign each animation block an animation delegate that responds when the animation triggers key events such as animationDidStop. Let's start with an example, and then we'll dissect the animation block and have a look at all of the players involved.

```
1   - (void)viewDidLoad {
2       [super viewDidLoad];
3       UIView *box = [[UIView alloc] initWithFrame:
                                    CGRectMake(10, 10, 50, 50)];
```

```
4        box.backgroundColor = [UIColor blueColor];
5
6        [self.view addSubview:box];
7
8        [UIView beginAnimations:@"box-animate" context:nil];
9        [UIView setAnimationDuration:1];
10
11       box.backgroundColor = [UIColor redColor];
12       box.frame = CGRectMake(50, 50, 100, 100);
13       box.alpha = .5;
14
15       [UIView commitAnimations];
16
17       [box release];
18   }
```

This code block is a simple implementation of a viewDidLoad method inside a custom UIViewController. Our animation block starts at line 8 and ends at line 15. But let's stop and take a look at the setup.

First, in line 3 we create a UIView called box and initialize it with the frame (10, 10, 50, 50). Remember the CGRectMake function defines (x,y,width,height). So our UIView box is initialized with the top left corner at location (10,10) and has a height and width of 50. Next, we set the background color of our box to blue in line 4, and then add our box as a subview to the view associated with our UIViewController. At this point, our app simply shows a blue box on the screen (see illustration).

In line 8, we begin our animation block. Each animation can have a string identifier; in our case we called our animation "box-animate." In line 9, we set the animation duration of this block to one second.

You'll notice in lines 11 through 13 we start changing some of the properties of our original blue box: making it red, changing the frame, and decreasing the opacity. Because these changes are made within a UIView animation block, they won't happen until the animation block is committed. Finally, in line 15 we commit the animation block.

As soon as we commit the animation block, any changes that have been made to the animatable properties of the UIView that occurred between the beginAnimation method and the commitAnimation method automatically transition over the duration of the animation block. In our case, the blue box takes exactly one second to animate its color, position, and opacity to the new values set between lines 11 and 13. By the end of our animation, the blue box is no longer blue.

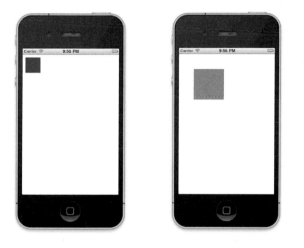

Before (left) and After (right) Animation

It's as easy as that! Creating animations using the APIs of UIKit are simple; you just have to remember these simple steps:

1. Create or define a UIView with some set of initial conditions.
2. Begin an animation block.
3. Configure the settings of your animation block including duration, repeat count, animation curve, and so on.
4. Make changes to your UI elements.
5. Commit the animation block to begin animating the transition between changes.

Get the Code ⟹ ⟹ ⟹

Go to **fromideatoapp.com/downloads/example#animatedemo** to download AnimationDemo and all of the project files including some that were not discussed in this chapter.

UIView Animation Methods

When setting up your UIView animation blocks, there are a few methods you should know (see Table 10.2). These are defined as a part of UIKit in the interface of UIView.

TABLE 10.2
UIView Animation Methods and Descriptions

Method	Description
setAnimationDelegate	Methods in the animation delegate are called based on the value of animationWillStartSelector and animationWillStopSelector. The delegate must be set for these functions to work properly
setAnimationWillStartSelector	The selector to call on the delegate when the animation starts
setAnimationDidStopSelector	The selector to call on the delegate when the animation finishes. This is useful if you want to change a series of animations together
setAnimationDuration	The duration, in seconds, of the animation block
setAnimationDelay	The delay, in seconds, between the time the commit block is reached and the time the animation begins. animationWillStart will not be called until after the delay
setAnimationStartDate	The start date of the animation. It allows you to schedule animations for a specific time in the future
setAnimationCurve	The animation curve. Options include linear, ease-in, ease-out, and ease-in-and-out. The default value is UIViewAnimationCurveEaseInOut
setAnimationRepeatCount	The number of times the animation block will repeat
setAnimationRepeatAutoreverses	A Boolean to determine if the animation should animate a reversal back to the state before the animation block
setAnimationBeginsFromCurrentState	If this value is set to YES, and you commit an animation on an object that is currently being animated, the original animation stops where it is and picks up the new animation. If this value is set to NO, the original animation finishes before starting the new animation.

Designer Note

Animation is an important part of the overall user experience. When designing mobile apps, particularly iOS apps, consider how your users will transition from screen to screen. Familiarize yourself with the animation methods outlined in Table 10.2 and consider how you might incorporate animation duration, repeat count, and other methods into the overall user experience.

Animating Between UIViews

An added benefit of working with the UIKit animation API is the ability to elegantly transition between alternating UIViews. Prior to iOS 4.0, developers had to use an additional method in the animation block: setAnimationTransition:forView:cache. By using animation transitions in the animation block, developers could leverage common iOS animations such as the page curl or the 3D flip effect seen in the native Weather app.

However, with the introduction of iOS 4.0, we now have more dedicated methods designed specifically for swapping out two UIViews. Consider the following code block:

```
1   - (void)flipToBack:(id)sender {
2       // Animate transition from frontView to backView
3   [UIView transitionFromView:frontView
                    toView:backView
                 duration:1
                  options:UIViewAnimationOptionTransitionFlipFromRight
               completion:nil];
4       }
```

Here we have a great example of how to use UIView animations. This method is set up to be the target of a button, for example, the Info button on the native Weather app. When this method is called, a single UIView animation is triggered. It looks like multiple lines of code because of the formatting, but we are really just setting multiple parameters of one UIView transition.

The first parameter is the transitionFromView. Here we identify the transitionFromView as frontView. We are assuming in this case that frontView is a UIView subclass that is currently visible on the screen. The second parameter, toView, is set to backView. Again, backView is assumed to be a UIView subclass, but in this case backView is a view that is not yet visible to the user. This animation will animate a transition between the frontView and the backView.

The duration and options parameters are self-explanatory. Essentially we are saying that the duration of the animation is one second, and the transition should happen using a 3D flip animation from the right. Here are some other options for the animation transition:

- UIViewAnimationOptionTransitionFlipFromLeft
- UIViewAnimationOptionTransitionFlipFromRight
- UIViewAnimationOptionTransitionCurlUp
- UIViewAnimationOptionTransitionCurlDown

Get the Code ➡ ➡ ➡

Go to **fromideatoapp.com/downloads/example#transitiondemo** to download TransitionDemo and all of the project files including some that were not discussed in this chapter.

System-Provided Animations

As I'm sure you have noticed, iOS methods often have a parameter called *animated*. When you set this parameter to YES, iOS performs the desired call automatically using an animation. These animated calls are all over the iOS SDK and it's a good idea to know where you can easily leverage animations in your designs to take advantage of work that is already done for you. Here are some of the more common animated calls in iOS development.

UIApplication

The UIApplication represents your application object in iOS and contains all of the necessary properties. A few of these properties can be hidden while your app is running. You find that oftentimes, if an object in iOS has a `setHidden` method, it usually has a `setHidden:animated:` method as well. Table 10.3 describes the UIApplication system-provided animations.

Method	Description
`setStatusBarOrientation:animated:`	Sets the status bar to specified orientation
`setStatusBarHidden:withAnimation:`	Hides or reveals the status bar using the animation style, UIStatusBarAnimationNone, UIStatusBarAnimationFade, or UIStatusBarAnimationSlide
`setStatusBarStyle:animated:`	Changes the status bar style to UIStatusBarStyleDefault, UIStatusBarStyleBlackTranslucent, or UIStatusBarStyleBlackOpaque
`setStatusBarHidden:animated:`	Hides the status bar, however, this function was deprecated in iOS 3.2. In iOS 4.0 and later, use setStatusBarHidden: withAnimation

TABLE 10.3
UIApplication System-Provided Animations

UIViewController

The UIViewController is truly a versatile class. Giving you complete control over the UIView and subviews, the UIViewController also contains numerous convenient methods for performing common tasks with animations. Table 10.4 describes the system-provided animations available to the UIViewController.

Method	Description
`presentModalViewController:animated:`	Present a modal view controller using the animation defined in modal view transition style
`dismissModalViewControllerAnimated:`	Dismiss a modal view controller according to the animation defined in modal view transition style
`setToolbarItems:animated:`	Animate (fade animation) new toolbar items onto the UIViewController's associated UIToolbar

TABLE 10.4
UIViewController System-Provided Animations

UITableView

The UITableViewController is a subclass of the UIViewController where the associated view is a UITableView. The UITableView defines a series of calls used for updating and managing itself. When reloading, inserting, or deleting UITableViewCells, iOS defines a UITableViewRowAnimation Style in one of the following ways:

- UITableViewRowAnimationFade
- UITableViewRowAnimationRight
- UITableViewRowAnimationLeft
- UITableViewRowAnimationTop
- UITableViewRowAnimationBottom
- UITableViewRowAnimationNone
- UITableViewRowAnimationMiddle

Table 10.5 presents UITableView system-provided animations.

TABLE 10.5
UITableView
System-Provided
Animations

Method	Description
scrollToRowAtIndexPath: atScrollPosition:animated:	Scroll the table view to the defined index path
scrollToNearestSelectedRow AtScrollPosition:animated:	Scroll the table view to the nearest selected row around a given scroll position
selectRowAtIndexPath: animated:scrollPosition:	Animate the selection of a row at the provided index path
deselectRowAtIndexPath: animated:	Animate the deselect of a row at the provided index path
insertRowsAtIndexPaths: withRowAnimation:	Insert rows using row animation
deleteRowsAtIndexPaths: withRowAnimation:	Delete rows using row animation
insertSections: withRowAnimation:	Insert a section using row animation
deleteSections: withRowAnimation:	Delete a section using row animation
reloadRowsAtIndexPaths: withRowAnimation:	Reload rows using row animation
reloadSections: withRowAnimation:	Reload sections using row animation
setEditing:animated:	Animate the transition to editing mode of the UITableView

UINavigationController

Finally, we'll look at one of the most recognizable iOS animations: the UINavigationController's push and slide navigation style. When we first talked about the UINavigationController back in Chapter 5, User Interface Controllers and Navigation, we talked briefly about the push and pop methods used to add new UIViewControllers to the navigation stack. The UINavigationController gives you a bit more control over the UINavigation stack, however, and of course provides you with easy access to animations along the way. Table 10.6 describes UINavigation-Controller system-provided animations.

Method	Description
pushViewController:animated:	Push a new UIViewController onto the navigation stack
popViewControllerAnimated:	Remove the top UIViewController from the navigation stack
popToRootViewControllerAnimated:	Animate the transition to the first UIViewController in the navigation stack. This removes all other view controllers and leaves only the remaining root view controller
popToViewController:animated:	Pop to a specific view controller in the navigation stack
setViewControllers:animated:	Populate the navigation stack with an array of view controllers
setNavigationBarHidden:animated:	Animate and toggle the hidden state of the UINavigationController's associated UINavigationBar
setToolbarHidden:animated:	Animate and toggle the hidden state of the UINavigationController's associated UIToolbar

TABLE 10.6
UINavigation-Controller System-Provided Animations

CHAPTER 11

Creating Custom iOS Animations

In the last chapter we learned how to animate the user interface using system-provided tools. By now, you should have a firm grasp of how to a design user interface and create user experience workflows that incorporate these system-provided animations.

So if the system-provided animations are so powerful, why would you ever need to build your own? By creating our own animations, we will not be bounded by the rules and restrictions of UIViews. Additionally, we will be able to do more complex keyframe animations, without the hassle of stringing together a series of animation blocks using animation *did stop* selectors.

Because the reasoning for incorporating custom animations in our designs is very similar to the reasoning behind using system-provided animations, this chapter will focus more on the technical side of the equation. While developers can walk away with an understanding of how to implement custom animations in code, I encourage designers to pay attention to the underlying features and capabilities you will be able to incorporate by leveraging Core Animations.

About Core Animation

We will build our own animations using a system framework called Core Animation. Just as overriding drawRect through Core Graphics gives us the ability to draw directly on the UIView and change its appearance (see Chapter 10), Core Animation provides extended control when it comes to animating custom views. This system-level framework lets us animate the properties defined in UIView as well as those defined in the Core Animation layer. Further, it allows us to easily create keyframe animations and apply 3D transforms to 2D layers.

It is important to understand the difference between what can be done with UIKit API animations and what can be done using Core Animation directly. Core Animation powers the animations provided by the UIKit API, so there are few direct performance differences between the two techniques. Because the UIKit API animation is defined in the UIView class, however, it is limited by the properties and capabilities of a UIView. Core Animation, on the other hand, interacts directly with the Core Animation layer of a view, giving you more power when it comes to animations.

In this chapter, we'll discuss three uses of Core Animation:

- Animating properties not defined in UIView
- Performing a 3D transformation on a 2D layer
- Animating a layer using a series of keyframe and path animations

As an iOS designer or developer, when you design a new UI or UX workflow, it's not necessarily critical to know up front whether a given animation will be implemented using Core Animation or UIKit APIs. It is important, however, to understand the different capabilities of each technique. You'll find that through Core Animation, you can create animations that appear to be complicated, but which are, in fact, quite simple to implement.

Take, for example, a custom animation that Apple created for the Mail app on the iPhone and iPod touch using Core Animation: when the user moves a message from the inbox to another folder, an email icon moves along an arc into the target folder. It's small things like this that will make the user step back and say, "Wow!" and ultimately market your app for you via word-of-mouth.

Mail App
Move Message
Animation

Key Differences with Core Animation

Because Core Animation operates at a lower level than the UIKit API animations, there are a few key differences to be aware of. The first is the Core Animation layer, or CALayer. A layer is much like a view; both define a set of properties that make up what is eventually displayed on the screen. In fact, every UIView has a layer property that is used as a low-level representation of that view. Up to this point, we've set properties like the frame and opacity on the UIView. When we do this, iOS also sets those properties on the view's underlying CALayer, which is eventually rendered to the user.

Because we're working with layers instead of views, we can animate the properties of the layer using Core Animation. As of iOS 4.2, there are over 26 separate properties in the CALayer class that can be animated with Core Animation. Some key properties that are not available in UIKit animations are anchor point for rotation, corner radius, mask layers, and shadows.

Another key difference between Core Animation and UIKit animations is the Core Animation class, or CAAnimation. Core Animation defines a subset of animation classes that is used when implementing animations. An animation class is an object that defines the distinct properties of that particular animation. Using these classes, you can animate or transition an entire layer or specific properties of a layer using basic or keyframe animations.

Developer Note

This book only touches on the power of Core Animation. You can visit **fromideatoapp.com/reference#core-animation** for a complete list of the animatable properties of a CALayer, as well as tutorials and more examples involving Core Animation. Additionally, because Core Animation is a low-level API in iOS, the same techniques are used to implement animations in Mac OS X. iOS and Mac developers can go to **developer.apple.com** for extensive documentation on Core Animation.

Core Animation Types

When working with Core Animation, there are three different types of Core Animation classes that you will deal with often:

- CABasicAnimation
- CAKeyframeAnimation
- CATransitionAnimation

Both CABasicAnimation and CAKeyframeAnimation are used to animate distinct properties in a layer. To transition an entire layer, you can use the CATransitionAnimation class. Multiple animations can be grouped together in a single animation class called CAAnimationGroup. For example, to change the size and opacity of a layer, you would first create a CABasicAnimation for each property and then combine them into a single CAAnimationGroup. This group is then added to the CALayer you wish to animate.

Implicit vs. Explicit Animations

There are two types of animations within the Core Animation framework: implicit and explicit. Unlike UIViews, the CALayer actually contains a presentation layer and a model layer. The presentation layer is used when displaying the layer on the screen and is optimized accordingly. The model layer is used to store the necessary layer information in memory.

If an animation is implicit, it means that the values being animated are stored in both the presentation layer and the model layer. If an animation is explicit, the values being animated are stored only in the presentation layer; the model layer remains untouched. This means that unless action is otherwise taken, after an explicit animation has completed, the CALayer reverts to its pre-animated state because the underlying model layer is not modified.

This distinction allows for further performance enhancements in iOS. For example, if you have an animation that is continuous (e.g., a spinning icon or image), it is more efficient to use explicit animations so that iOS doesn't waste resources by changing the underlying model layer. Since the view is always animating, we really care only about the changes in the presentation layer. Additionally, for complicated animation groups or paths, you can use explicit animations to interpolate values over the duration of the animation, and then set the implicit values in the model when the animation is complete.

Developer Note

This chapter talks primarily about using the CAAnimation class for controlling animations, which are, in fact, explicit animations. Go to **fromideatoapp.com/reference#implicit-animations** to learn more about implicit animations.

Getting Started with Core Animations

To create a new animation using Core Animation, you need to follow three simple steps. Before you start, however, make sure the Quartz-Core framework has been added to your project in Xcode. Because Xcode only automatically includes the UIKit and UIFoundation libraries, you'll need to link the Quartz framework to your project.

Importing the Quartz Library to Xcode

To include the Quartz library in your project, start by choosing *Project > Edit Active Target "your project name"* in the Xcode menu bar. In the General tab of the Info dialog, click the Plus button located at the bottom left of the window. Next, select QuartzCore.framework from the list and click the Add button.

Adding Quartz
Library to Your
Project

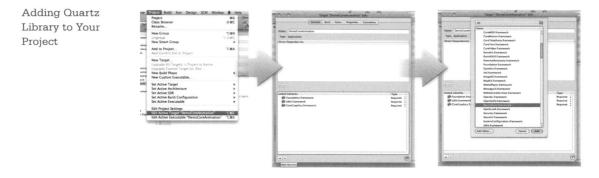

After the Quartz library is included, add the following line of code to the top of the header file (.h) in the custom UIView that will implement Core Animation.

```
1  #import <QuartzCore/QuartzCore.h>
```

Animating an Object with Core Animation

Now that our project is set up to use the QuartzCore library, we can start referencing Core Animation. As mentioned earlier, there are three simple steps to creating your first animation using the Core Animation framework:

1. Create a new reference to a CAAnimation or CAAnimation subclass.

2. Define the properties of your CAAnimation.

3. Assign your animation to a layer.

Once you assign the CAAnimation to your layer, iOS automatically handles the execution of the animation on a separate thread. Let's take a look at an example. In the following code block, we'll animate our custom UIView's background color to blue and then back to its original color.

```
1  CABasicAnimation *animation = [CABasicAnimation animation];
2  animation.toValue = (id)[UIColor blueColor].CGColor;
3  animation.duration = 1;
4  animation.autoreverses = YES;
5  [self.layer addAnimation:animation forKey:@"backgroundColor"];
```

In line 1, we create a new CABasicAnimation object. In line 2, we set the `toValue` property, which defines where we want to end up; in our case, we want to end up with a value of the color blue. In lines 3 and 4, we set the `duration` of the animation in seconds and set the `autoreverses` property to YES. This means our view will animate over one second to change blue and then automatically reverse the animation back to the original color for an additional one second. Finally, in line 5, we add the animation to the layer using the key "backgroundColor."

The `forKey` parameter in line 5 is actually very important. The key defined in this parameter should be the same name as the variable you're trying to animate. If you are trying to set a specific variable like the width of your view, you can use dot syntax to reference sub-variables in a structure. For example, if you wanted to set the width of your view by adjusting the bounds, you would use

```
1   [self.layer addAnimation:animation forKey:@"bounds.size.width"];
```

In this code block, we animate the width property of the bounds by referencing "bounds.size.width" in the key parameter.

Get the Code ➭ ➭ ➭

Go to **fromideatoapp.com/download/examples#core-animation-demo** to download this sample project along with other Core Animation effects.

Keyframe Animations

We just saw examples of creating basic property animations. Besides gaining the ability to animate layer properties that are unavailable in UIKit animations, you probably noticed that the capabilities of basic animation aren't much different from those of UIKit animation. Keyframe animations change all of that.

A keyframe animation is a basic animation in which you define key steps (or frames) along the way. To do this in UIKit, you would have to implement a series of `setAnimationDidStopSelector` methods to daisy chain a series of animation blocks together. With keyframe animations in Core Animation, you can accomplish the same goal with only a few lines of code.

Let's take the same color change example, but this time let's animate to green and yellow before we animate to blue.

```
1  CAKeyframeAnimation *animation = [CAKeyframeAnimation animation];
2  animation.values = [NSArray arrayWithObjects:
                            (id)self.layer.backgroundColor,
                            (id)[UIColor yellowColor].CGColor,
                            (id)[UIColor greenColor].CGColor,
                            (id)[UIColor blueColor].CGColor,nil];
3  animation.duration = 3;
4  animation.autoreverses = YES;
5  [self.layer addAnimation:animation forKey:@"backgroundColor"];
```

You'll notice in this code block, we really only changed a few lines of code. In line 1, instead of creating a CABasicAnimation, we created a CAKeyframeAnimation. Similarly, instead of assigning a toValue in line 2, we assigned an array of values to the property values. Each value in this array will be used as a keyframe, or step value, in the animation. Lines 3 through 5 are much the same. We set the animation duration, define autoreverses, and then add the animation to our layer using the key "backgroundColor."

Get the Code ➟ ➟ ➟

Go to **fromideatoapp.com/download/examples#core-animation-demo** to download this sample project along with other Core Animation effects.

> **>_**
>
> **Developer Note**
>
> Notice how the first value in the values array refers to the current color of the layer **self.layer.backgroundColor.** When a keyframe animation is started, the first value in the values array is used as the initial condition for the animation. To prevent the animation from abruptly changing the initial color, we pull the current value from the model layer of our view's associated CALayer. That way, when the animation starts, the current layer transitions seamlessly into the first keyframe.

Animating Along Paths

In addition to animating a CAKeyframeAnimation through a series of
values, you can animate a keyframe animation along a specified path.
The following code sample creates the email animation that we discussed earlier in the chapter.

```
1   CAKeyframeAnimation *ani = [CAKeyframeAnimation animation];
2   CGMutablePathRef aPath = CGPathCreateMutable();
3   CGPathMoveToPoint(aPath, nil, 20, 20);          //Origin Point
4   CGPathAddCurveToPoint(aPath, nil, 160, 30,      //Control Point 1
                                      220, 220,     //Control Point 2
                                      240, 380);    //End Point
5   ani.path = aPath;
6   ani.duration = 1;
7   ani.timingFunction = [CAMediaTimingFunction
        functionWithName:kCAMediaTimingFunctionEaseIn];
8   ani.rotationMode = @"auto";
9   [ball.layer addAnimation:ani forKey:@"position"];
10  CFRelease(aPath);
```

Once again, we create a CAKeyframeAnimation in line 1. In line 2, we
start creating the custom path that will eventually be our animation
path. In lines 3 and 4, we construct the path using an origin point of
(20,20), a curve with control points of (160,30) and (220,220), and an
endpoint of (240,380). The origin, control points, and endpoints work
together to make a smooth curve in our CALayer. To help you visualize
the curve, let's look at where these points fall in our canvas:

Custom Path
Built With Control
Points

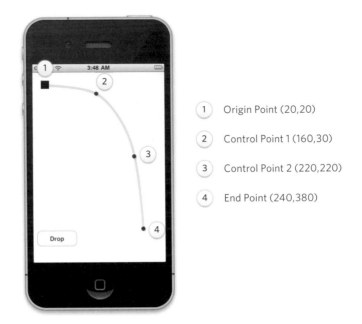

1 Origin Point (20,20)

2 Control Point 1 (160,30)

3 Control Point 2 (220,220)

4 End Point (240,380)

As you can see from this figure, iOS automatically connects the control points to form a smooth curve, which results in our desired path.

Next, in line 5, we apply the path to our animation, and in line 6 we set the animation duration. In line 7, we set the timing function, which controls how an animation moves throughout the animation. This example uses the `Ease In` timing function, which means that the animation will move slowly at the beginning and then accelerate toward the end—exactly the kind of behavior we want in our box-dropping effect. Other timing functions include `Linear`, `EaseOut`, and `EaseInEaseOut`.

Line 8 is unique to the keyframe animation. The `rotateMode` of a key-frame animation controls how the layer reacts to changes in direction along the path. By setting this value to `auto`, the layer automatically rotates relative to the path. Again, it is a small detail, but one that really sells the dropping effect we're creating. In lines 9 and 10, we add the animation and clean up some memory.

Get the Code ⇨ ⇨ ⇨

Go to **fromideatoapp.com/download/examples#mail-app-drop** to download a sample project including a demonstration of the Mail app drop animation.

> ### Designer Note
>
> From a designer's point of view, there are a few things that a developer can benefit from knowing in advance. Take, for example, the drop effect we created to emulate the email animation in the Mail app. It's much easier for the designer to define the path and control points of a given animation than for the developers to implement it themselves. If, as a designer, you define the animation parameters and animation paths, you will improve the quality and consistency of your design, as well as the final product.

Animation Transitions

The next CAAnimation class we'll discuss is the CATransition class. CATransitions are used to transition the entire layer—not just an individual property. Fortunately, CATransitions are very straightforward and have only two properties that you need to worry about: type and subtype. The type of transition determines the transition effect your layer will use. There are four options, which are described in Table 11.1.

TABLE 11.1 CATransition Types

Transition Type	Description
kCATransitionFade	The current layer fades out with the new layer or modified layer beneath. With this transition type, the subtype is ignored
kCATransitionMoveIn	The new layer or modified layer moves in from the direction defined in the subtype property. The new layer moves in on top of the old layer
kCATransitionPush	The new layer or modified layer pushes in from the direction defined in the subtype property. The old layer is pushed out in the direction opposite of that defined in the subtype layer
kCATransitionReveal	The current layer moves off-screen in the direction opposite of that defined in the subtype property, revealing the new layer or modified layer beneath

The subtype of a transition changes the direction in which the CATransition moves. There are four subtypes defined for the CATransition class:

■ kCATransitionFromRight

■ kCATransitionFromLeft

■ kCATransitionFromTop

■ kCATransitionFromBottom

The following code block demonstrates how to use the CATransition animation class. Here we'll take our existing custom UIView and apply a transition style to the layer.

```
1  CATransition *trans = [CATransition animation];
2  trans.type = kCATransitionReveal;
3  trans.subtype = kCATransitionFromLeft;
4  trans.duration = .5;
5  [self.layer addAnimation:trans forKey:@"transition"];
6  self.layer.backgroundColor = [UIColor blueColor].CGColor;
```

This code block does something a bit different than the previous ones. Remember the difference between implicit and explicit animations. In this code block, we actually modify both the presentation layer and the model layer for our CALayer class. Because CATransitions transitions between two layers, we modify the model of the current layer just after adding the animation. The result is that the animation uses the last-known presentation layer, and the layer revealed is the newly defined model layer.

In line 1, we create our new CATransition object, then, in lines 2 and 3, we set the type and subtype properties. We add our animation to the layer in line 5, and then make an implicit change to the layer's model in line 6.

Get the Code ⇒ ⇒ ⇒

Go to **fromideatoapp.com/download/examples#core-animation-demo** to download this sample project along with other Core Animation effects.

3D Transforms

Core Animation lets you apply a 3D transform matrix to your layers, making it possible to transform a flat layer in 3D space. This does not mean that iOS will add a third dimension to your layer, but rather that you can easily manipulate the view as if it existed in a 3D environment. Both rotation and position can be manipulated on all three axes: x, y, and z. With this capability, you can easily implement or produce a custom 3D flip animation like the one created in the `transitionFromView` method described in Chapter 10, Introduction to iOS Animations.

UIKit animations allow you to rotate an object along the plane parallel with the surface of the screen. By using 3D transforms, however, you can flip your views along the x-, y-, or z-axis, or any combination thereof. The following code sample shows the steps necessary to implement the same 3D card flip seen in the default Weather app on the iPhone and iPod touch:

1. Create a CABasicAnimation to rotate or spin the layer along the y-axis (vertical).

2. Create a CABasicAnimation to scale down the card to enhance the 3D effect.

3. Combine the flip and scale animations into a single CAGroupAnimation.

4. Apply the group animation to the layer.

Note

In this method, we create animations with the **animationWithKeyPath** method. This allows us to assign the animation key when we first create the animation class, rather than at the end when we add the animation to the layer.

```
1    //Step 1: Create basic y-axis rotation animation
2    CABasicAnimation *flip = [CABasicAnimation
         animationWithKeyPath:@"transform.rotation.y"];
3    flip.toValue = [NSNumber numberWithDouble:-M_PI];
4
5    //Step 2: Create basic scale animation
6    CABasicAnimation *scale = [CABasicAnimation
         animationWithKeyPath:@"transform.scale"];
7    scale.toValue = [NSNumber numberWithDouble:.9];
8    scale.duration = .5;
9    scale.autoreverses = YES;
10
```

```
11  //Step 3: Combine scale and flip into one animation group
12  CAAnimationGroup *group = [CAAnimationGroup animation];
13  group.animations = [NSArray arrayWithObjects:flip, scale, nil];
14  group.timingFunction = [CAMediaTimingFunction
        functionWithName:kCAMediaTimingFunctionEaseInEaseOut];
15  group.duration = 1;
16  group.fillMode = kCAFillModeForwards;
17  group.removedOnCompletion = NO;
18
19  //Step 4: Add animation group to our layer
20  [self.layer addAnimation:group forKey:@"flip"];
```

And just like that, we have our own custom 3D card flip animation! Remember the steps we implemented in this code block were:

1. **Lines 2–3:** Create a CABasicAnimation to flip the layer along the y-axis.

2. **Lines 6–9:** Create a CABasicAnimation to scale down the card to enhance the 3D effect.

3. **Lines 12–17:** Combine the flip and scale animations into a single CAGroupAnimation.

4. **Line 20:** Apply the group animation to the layer.

Get the Code ⟫ ⟫ ⟫

Go to **fromideatoapp.com/download/examples#core-animation-demo** to download this sample project along with other Core Animation effects.

iOS App Blueprint

Custom Animations

In Part IV, Animating Your UI, we talked about how to incorporate custom animations in our UIViews and UIViewControllers. While the last few chapters included many examples, let's take a look at how we can incorporate some of these animations into our progressive blueprint app. To get started, go to **fromideatoapp.com/downloads/ blueprint4_assets.zip** to download the image files and the special UIViewController subclass named CountdownViewController.

Get the Code ➡ ➡ ➡

This blueprint involves a lot of code and the creation of files. If you get lost, or feel more comfortable following along with a completed project, go to **fromideatoapp.com/downloads/blueprints** to download FI2ADemo.

Overview

In this blueprint we're going to incorporate a custom UIViewController called CountdownViewController. This is actually a custom UIView-Controller class that I created for a few of my apps with Kelby Training, and I've found that it works quite well.

The CountdownViewController class is simple. The view controller itself is initialized with a number to start counting down from and a delegate to handle the countdown control events. The countdown control events that must be implemented by the delegate are countdownDidStart, countdownDidFinish, and countdownDidCancel. In most cases, the delegate is simply the controller that created the countdown.

We'll modify our T2_TableViewController class so that when a row is selected, the controller presents a new CountdownViewController. For simplicity's sake, we'll assume that the first row in the table is two seconds, the second row is four seconds, the next row is six seconds, and so on. The row you select will determine the starting count number.

To implement the CountdownViewController, we'll perform the following steps:

1. Copy the folder Countdown (from the zip file blueprint4_assets.zip) into the Classes folder. Copy the image closebox.png into our app resources.
2. Implement the delegate methods of CountdownViewController.
3. Implement the didSelectRowAtIndexPath method in T2_TableViewController to present the countdown timer.

Step 1

Download the blueprint assets at **fromideatoapp.com/downloads/ blueprint4_assets.zip**, then unzip the zip file and drag the Countdown folder into your Classes folder in Xcode and the image closebox. png to your app resources in Xcode. When asked, copy the files to the destination's group folder. This folder contains two classes: one a subclass of UIView, and the other a subclass of UIViewController. We'll use the closebox.png image as a Cancel button for our countdown.

The UIView subclass is called HUDView. HUDView is a very simple class that draws a rectangle with rounded corners at 66 percent opacity.

(We learned how to do this in Chapter 8, Creating Custom UIViews and UIViewControllers.) When our UIViewController subclass Count-downViewController is initialized, instead of using a nib or viewDid-Load, CountdownViewController associates itself with its own view (in this case, an instance of HUDView) using the loadView method. As a result, when you create a new instance of CountdownViewController, the view of this view controller is automatically a rounded rectangle with 66 percent opacity—perfect for our Heads Up Display (HUD).

Step 2

Now that we have our class files included in the project, we need to import them on our T2_TableViewController header file. Addition-ally, we need to identify to Xcode that T2_TableViewController will conform to the protocol for a CountdownViewControllerDelegate. This means T2_TableViewController will implement the countdownDidStart, countdownDidFinish, and countdownDidCancel methods.

We need to make only two changes in our header file to include Count-downViewController and conform to CountdownViewControllerDelegate:

```
1   #import <UIKit/UIKit.h>
2   #import "CountdownViewController.h"
3
4   @interface T2_TableViewController : UITableViewController
        <CountdownViewControllerDelegate> {
5
6   }
7
8   @end
```

In line 2, we import CountdownViewController.h, and in line 4 we include <CountdownViewControllerDelegate> between the subclass and the first right brace to conform to the delegate protocol. Now we're ready to implement the actual CountdownViewController delegate methods.

We'll add the following code block to the T2_TableViewController.m file:

```
1   ////////////////////////////////
2   // Countdown Delegate Methods //
3   ////////////////////////////////
4   - (void)countdownDidStart:(CountdownViewController *)countdown{
5       self.tableView.allowsSelection = NO;
6   }
7
8   - (void)countdownDidCancel:(CountdownViewController *)countdown{
9       [countdown dismissCountdown:YES];
10      self.tableView.allowsSelection = YES;
11  }
12  - (void)countdownDidFinish:(CountdownViewController *)countdown{
13      [countdown dismissCountdown:YES];
14      self.tableView.allowsSelection = YES;
15  }
```

When the CountdownViewController calls its delegate methods, it does so while providing a reference to itself. This comes in handy because we can choose to dismiss the controller or restart it depending on the circumstances. In the first method, shown in lines 4 through 6, we implement the countdownDidStart method. Because selecting a row in our UITableView starts a new timer, we want to turn off selection in our table view when the timer first begins. In the second method, shown in lines 8 through 10, we handle a case where the timer was canceled. In line 9, we dismiss the timer using an animated Boolean operator, and turn table selection back on. Finally, in lines 12 through 14, we handle a case where the timer finishes normally. Again, we dismiss the timer in line 13, and turn our tableView's selection back on.

Step 3

Next, we create and present a new CountdownViewController. Do so by implementing the didSelectRowAtIndexPath method in the T2_TableViewController:

```
1   - (void)tableView:(UITableView *)tableView
      didSelectRowAtIndexPath:(NSIndexPath *)indexPath {
2
3       //Create a new countdown
4       // Initialize with (Row+1)*2 (because rows are zero-indexed)
5       // Set self as the delegate
6       CountdownViewController *count = [[CountdownViewController alloc]
            initWithCount:(indexPath.row+1)*2
            withDelegate:self];
7
8       // Configure our countdown text settings
9       count.textLabel.text = @"Counting Down!";
10      count.detailLabel.text = [NSString
            stringWithFormat:@"You selected %d seconds",
                    (indexPath.row+1)*2];
11
12      //Present the countdown in the view of our navigation controller
13      [count presentInView:self.navigationController.view animated:YES];
15      [count release];
16
17  }
```

Here we have the didSelectRowAtIndexPath method of T2_TableView-
Controller. This method is called whenever a row is selected on the
table view. In line 6, we create a new countdown controller using twice
the row value (plus 1 because our rows are zero-index) as a starting
count, and then the delegate as self. Remember, we just finished implementing the delegate methods. Next, in lines 9 and 10, we configure the
text label settings of our countdown timer, and then finally, in line 13,
we present the countdown timer in the view of the navigation controller.

Why did we present the timer in the navigation controller's view?
Because self is a UITableViewController, self.view is a subclass of

UIScrollView, meaning that it scrolls. If we presented the countdown timer in self.view, we'd be able to scroll the timer off the screen. This is not what we want with a heads up display.

Animations of CountdownViewController

CountdownViewController is a great example of how to use animations well in your apps. Notice that when the timer is presented on the screen, it zooms in as if popped on top of the screen. This effect is created using the standard UIView animation blocks we learned about in Chapter 10, Introduction to iOS Animations. Let's look at the code:

```
1   - (void)presentInView:(UIView *)view
               animated:(BOOL)animated{

2

3       if(animated){
4           // If our animated Boolean is YES
5           // set the initial conditions of our view
6           // at 3x scale, centered, with 0 opacity
7           CGAffineTransform t = self.view.transform;
8           self.view.transform = CGAffineTransformScale(t, 3.0, 3.0);
9           self.view.center = view.center;
10          self.view.alpha = 0;

11

12          // Because animated Boolean is YES, start our animation block
13          // and set our scale back to 1 (this will be animated)
14          [UIView beginAnimations:@"present-countdown" context:nil];
15          [UIView setAnimationDuration:.33];
16          [UIView setAnimationCurve:UIViewAnimationCurveEaseOut];
17          [UIView setAnimationDelegate:self];
18          [UIView setAnimationDidStopSelector:
                   @selector(presentAnimationDidStop)];

19

20          self.view.transform = CGAffineTransformScale(t, 1, 1);
21      }
```

```
22
23        // Define the final position and opacity of our view.
24        // If the animation block was animated, these values
25        // will be within the animation block and they
26        // will be animated to from our initial conditions.
27        // If the animated Boolean is NO, the animation block is
28        // skipped and these values become the new initial (and final)
29        // conditions for our view
30
31        self.view.center = view.center;
32        self.view.alpha = 1;
33        [view addSubview:self.view];
34
35        // If the animated Boolean was YES, commit the animation block
36        if(animated)
37            [UIView commitAnimations];
38 }
```

You'll notice we do something interesting here to implement a conditional animation. The method presentInView:animated: allows for the Boolean value animated to determine if the countdown timer should be added to the screen with or without animation. To accomplish this, we split the animation block into two pieces.

First, look what happens in this function if the animated Boolean value is set to NO. The first code isn't executed until line 31, where we set up the final appearance of the view. Because the start of the animation block is wrapped in an if statement, it is never started, so the view never animates.

Now consider if the animated Boolean value is set to YES. The first line of code that's executed now is line 7. Here we set up our view to be three times its normal size, with an opacity of zero. We also start the first half of our animation block, as seen in lines 14 through 18.

We know that the animation block automatically animates between values located just before the animation block and those values defined inside the animation block. If the animated Boolean value is set to NO, the animation block never starts, so the initial conditions are the ending point (lines 31 through 33). If the animation Boolean value is set to YES, the view receives a new set of initial conditions (lines 7 through 10) and then animates to our ending point (lines 31 through 33). This is just one of the practical examples of how you can use animations in your apps.

Get the Code ⇒ ⇒ ⇒

CountdownViewController implements a few different types of animations, including the dismissal of the view and the animation of the clock itself. Download FI2ADemo at **fromideatoapp.com/downloads/ blueprints** to see these examples and more.

Human Interaction: Gestures

CHAPTER 12

Introduction to iOS Gestures

What is a gesture? More importantly, why do gestures matter when designing user experience for mobile apps? We've talked about designing the user interface, looked at various iOS navigation metaphors, detailed the abundance of user interface elements at your disposal, and tied it all together with beautiful animations. But in the end, it all circles back to human interaction; the biggest difference between apps for iOS devices and apps for web pages or desktop computers boils down to gestures—how a user interacts with iOS apps and iOS hardware (recall our HID discussion in Chapter 3, Physical Hardware).

Apps respond to gestures, not clicks.

This is one of the fundamental principles outlined in Apple's Human Interface Guidelines. Desktop computer applications respond to keyboard input, mouse clicks, and so on. iOS apps respond to gestures, such as taps, drags, flicks, and swipes—all of which are formally defined by iOS. As you might expect, along with these definitions come expected behaviors. It is important that your apps implement gestures in a way that is consistent across the iOS environment.

Understanding Apple-Defined Gestures

To provide consistency across iOS apps, Apple has defined standard gestures and their expected behaviors. It is important to follow these guidelines when designing your apps, as users are already familiar with each gesture's use and behavior, based on their experience with built-in apps such as SMS, Photos, Maps, and Mail. Apple's predefined gestures are:

- Tap
- Drag
- Flick
- Swipe
- Double-Tap
- Pinch Open/Pinch Close
- Touch and Hold
- Shake

Note

This list includes only Apple-defined gestures with expected behaviors. It is possible to implement additional gestures where Apple has not yet defined an expected behavior such as a triple tap or two-finger swipe. We'll discuss how to implement custom gestures in Chapter 13, Creating Custom iOS Gestures.

Tap

The single-finger tap is one of the most intuitive gestures on an iOS device. Analogous to a mouse click on a desktop computer, a tap is a brief touch of the screen that is used to select, highlight, or control a UI element.

Drag

A single-finger drag is used to scroll or pan a view on the screen. The drag gesture tracks the location of the user's finger on the screen and moves the underlying UI object accordingly. A drag is commonly used to fine-tune the position of an object, such as a photo or UIScrollView.

A single tap gesture triggered by a one touch tap

Single-finger drag gesture triggered by a single finger's continuous movement and touch

Flick

Not to be confused with a drag, a flick is a single-finger gesture that is used to quickly scroll or pan a view. The iPhone introduced the concept of inertia scrolling. This means that when the user flicks the screen, instead of stopping immediately when the user's finger lifts up, the view continues to scroll and decelerates slowly to a stop. This enables the user to quickly and intuitively flick through a long list or to navigate paginated scroll views, such as the iOS home screen.

Swipe

Triggered by a sliding action, a single-finger swipe reveals additional functions of an element. While the drag and flick gestures can be used to navigate a UIScrollView or interact with a specific object, a swipe is used only for interaction. A swipe is commonly used with UITableView-Cells to reveal a Delete button, Reply button, or other options specific to that app or task.

Flick gesture caused by a short and deliberate directional touch

Swipe gesture triggered by a deliberate directional touch (longer than a flick, but not continuous)

Double-Tap

Double-tap means that the user quickly touches the screen twice in the same location (analogous to a double click). This gesture is used to automatically zoom in or zoom out on an image or UIScrollView. In the Photos app, it is used to focus in on an area of a photo. If a UIScroll-View has zooming enabled, the double-tap gesture allows the user to quickly zoom to a predetermined scale.

Pinch Open / Pinch Close

Pinch open and pinch close control the zoom on UIScrollView content. In the Photos app, these gestures enable the user to zoom in and out on an image. In the Safari app, they let the user zoom in and out on a web page. As of iOS 4.2, pinch to zoom is the only multifinger gesture defined by Apple's Human Interface Guidelines.

Double-Tap and Pinch Open / Pinch Close Gestures

Double tap gesture triggered by two quick touches in the same location

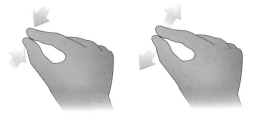

Pinch open and pinch close gesture triggered by two finger pinching motion

Touch and Hold

The touch and hold gesture is used to fine-tune text selection and cursor position on text elements. When the user presses and holds in editable text, iOS shows a magnified view of the cursor position. When the same action is performed on a web page or selectable text, iOS provides controls to select or copy text. The touch and hold gesture also presents a list of actions that can be taken on an object (presented in a UIActionSheet); for example, in Safari, it lets the user open links in a new window, copy images, or call a phone number.

Shake

In iOS 3.0, Apple introduced shake to undo, a standard across iOS apps. When an iOS device is physically shaken, it triggers a shake event that can be caught by an app. You can use this information to implement an undo action in your apps. Apple has automatically built in shake to undo typing for editable text in UITextFields and UITextViews.

Touch and Hold, and Shake Gesture

Touch and hold triggered by tapping and holding for a set period of time

Shake gesture triggered by shaking an iOS device

Gestures and UIKit

Many of the UI elements in UIKit are ready to go out of the box. For the most part, you won't need to do any extra development to implement gestures; simply design your app's workflows around incorporating them. Because buttons, sliders, inputs, and controls are all subclasses of the parent class UIControl, these elements automatically respond to tap or drag gestures accordingly using UIControlEvents. (See the Controls and Buttons section of Chapter 6, User Interface Buttons, Inputs, Indicators, and Controls). Similarly, because UITableViews inherit their properties from the UIScrollView class, scrolling in a table is also included automatically.

There are, however, a few options you can configure to enable or disable these gestures, if for some reason they are not needed or desired. For example, just because the UITableView can be configured to swipe and delete rows doesn't mean you want your table view to show a Delete button every time it's swiped.

In Chapter 9, Creating Custom Table Views, we focused on how to create and configure custom table views and UITableViewControllers. Now we'll learn how to configure specific gesture interactions on the UIScrollView parent class. As a designer, you should be mindful of the gestures your UI elements should and should not respond to.

> **Designer Note**
>
> It's important that gestures behave as users expect them to in your apps, but it's also important to remember that not every user will know when to use a particular gesture. When possible, provide an alternate means to accomplish each task. Consider the Mail app, for example: the user can swipe to delete a message, or tap the Edit button, select a row, and then press Delete. Strive to find a balance between intuitive gestures and obvious controls in your apps.

UIScrollView Gestures

As discussed in Chapter 4, Basic User Interface Objects, the UIScroll-View is a special class used to display content that is larger than the bounds of the scroll view. Simply put, the scroll view lets the user zoom and pan another view. The Maps app is a great example of a UIScroll-View: the user can drag a finger to reposition the map, pinch open and pinch close to control the level of zoom, and double-tap to quickly zoom in and out.

All of these interactions are built-in behaviors of the UIScrollView. But what do you need to know about these behaviors to configure them in your apps? First, let's take a step back and look at the UIScrollView again.

Scrolling and Panning a UIScrollView

When a user drags a finger within a UIScrollView, the content view subview is repositioned automatically. You can manage the panning behavior of the UIScrollView using the properties described in Table 12.1.

Property	Description
scrollEnabled	This Boolean value determines whether or not the scroll view allows scrolling. If disabled, the scroll view ignores any drag gestures
directionLockEnabled	If enabled, this Boolean value forces the scroll view to scroll one direction at a time. For example, if enabled, a user who starts scrolling up or down is locked into an up/down scroll until dragging ends
scrollsToTop	If enabled, this Boolean value allows a user to tap the status bar located at the top of the screen to automatically scroll the scroll view to the top
pagingEnabled	When paging is enabled, the content offset automatically positions itself at multiples of the bounds of the scroll view. The best example of this is the iOS Home screen with app icons. The app Home screen can be seen as one big UIScrollView with paging enabled. Because paging is enabled, the scroll view automatically positions itself on a page of icons as the user moves left and right, instead of stopping halfway between pages. Another example is flicking through full-screen images in the Photos app
bounces	When the bounces Boolean property is enabled, the scroll view lets the user scroll a little bit beyond the edge of the content view, but automatically animates a rubber band effect to bounce the user back to the edge. It's usually a good idea to leave this property enabled
alwaysBounceVertical	Allows the user to control edge bounces in the vertical direction
alwaysBounceHorizontal	Allows the user to control edge bounces in the horizontal direction
indicatorStyle	The scroll view indicators are like scroll bars in desktop applications. You can define the scroll view indicators to be black or white. Select the color that provides the highest contrast, to be visible in the context of your app
showsHorizontalScrollIndicator	This Boolean property defines whether or not the horizontal scroll indicator is visible
showsVerticalScrollIndicator	This Boolean property defines whether or not the vertical scroll indicator is visible
flashScrollIndicators	This method animates scroll indicators on-screen and then off-screen (if enabled)

TABLE 12.1
UIScrollView
Properties:
Scrolling Behaviors

Developer Note

Whenever you implement a UIScrollView or UITableView, it's a good idea to call the `flashScrollIndicators` in the `viewDid Appear:` method of your UIViewController. This provides important visual feedback to your users that the scroll view contains information that is not visible on the screen.

Zooming in UIScrollView

Apple's Human Interface Guidelines define two gestures that control the zoom function of a UIScrollView:

- Pinch Open / Pinch Close
- Double-Tap to Zoom

Note

You can easily implement pinch to zoom using delegate methods of the UIScrollView class. However, to implement double-tap to zoom, you'll need to implement a UIGestureRecognizer. We'll discuss how to use UIGestureRecognizers in Chapter 13, Creating Custom iOS Gestures.

Before you can allow zooming in your scroll view, you must first configure the properties of your scroll view as shown in Table 12.2.

TABLE 12.2
UIScrollView
Properties:
Zooming Behaviors

Property	Description
maximumZoomScale	This float value (decimal number) determines the maximum zoom scale of the content view. A maximumZoomScale of 2.0, and a content view of 100 x 100 would allow the UIScrollView to scale an image up to 200 x 200
minimumZoomScale	This float value (decimal number) determines the minimum zoom scale of the content view. A minimumZoomScale of .5 and a content view of 100 x 100 would allow the UIScrollView to scale an image down to 50 x 50
bouncesZoom	This Boolean value determines whether or not a user can zoom past the defined range and animate a rubber band bounce effect to snap back to the minimum or maximum zoom scale
contentSize	Of type CGSize, the contentSize property defines the height and width of the content of the scroll view

> **Developer Note**
>
> If needed, the UIScrollView provides control methods to pro-
> grammatically animate content zooming. You can choose either
> **zoomToRect:animated** or **setZoomScale:animated**. These methods
> can be very useful if your design calls for the user to zoom in on
> a default location on a map or image. For example, iOS uses these
> functions to automatically position the Maps app when geolocation
> is enabled.

You must define the four properties described in Table 12.2 before
zooming can be enabled in your scroll view. After you've configured the
scroll view with the required properties, you must tell the UIScroll-
View which view is actually being zoomed or panned. You can accomplish this by implementing the following method in your scroll view's
delegate:

```
1  - (UIView*)viewForZoomingInScrollView:(UIScrollView *)scrollView{
2       return myImage;
3  }
```

The above code block tells the scroll view to scale or reposition the
UIImageView, myImage, when scrolling and panning gestures are
made on the UIScrollView.

Our final code block should look something like this:

ScrollViewController.h

```
1  #import <UIKit/UIKit.h>
2  @interface ScrollViewController:UIViewController <UIScrollViewDelegate>{
3
4       UIScrollView *myScrollView;
5       UIImageView *myImage;
6
7       }
8  @end
```

In the code block above, we set up a ScrollViewController.h file. In line 2, notice that we have a new parameter in the interface declaration, <UIScrollViewDelegate>. This identifier tells iOS that this custom UIViewController class will implement the UIScrollView delegate methods. We must include this line of code if we want to set the delegate of the scroll view to self.

ScrollViewController.m

```
1   #import "ScrollViewController.h"
2   @implementation ScrollViewController
3   - (void)viewDidLoad {
4       [super viewDidLoad];
5       myImage = [[UIImageView alloc] initWithImage:
                                        [UIImage imageNamed:@"pic.png"]];
6
7       myScrollView = [[UIScrollView alloc]
                            initWithFrame:CGRectMake(0, 0, 320, 480)];
8       myScrollView.maximumZoomScale = 3;
9       myScrollView.minimumZoomScale = 1;
10      myScrollView.contentSize = myScrollView.frame.size;
11      myScrollView.delegate = self;
12
13      [myScrollView addSubview:myImage];
14
15  }
16  - (UIView*)viewForZoomingInScrollView:(UIScrollView *)scrollView{
17      return myImage;
18  }
```

In this second batch of code, we implement a ScrollViewController.m file. Here, we show the viewDidLoad method and the viewForZooming InScrollView: scroll view delegate method. When the scroll view is ready to zoom, it calls viewForZoomingInScrollView: on our delegate (currently set to self as seen in line 11).

In this case, we always return myImage as the scroll view's view for zooming. However, if we were creating a custom maps app, we could use this method to conditionally return a higher-resolution photo based on the current zoom level. If we were zoomed out, we could return a low-detail map. If we were zoomed in, we could return a high-detail map.

In the next chapter, we'll discuss how to implement double-tap to zoom by applying UIGestureRecognizers to our custom views.

Get the Code ➡➡➡

Go to **fromideatoapp.com/download/example#scrollviewgest** to download a project containing more examples from the UITapGestureRecognizer.

 Designer Note

Before your design is implemented, think through the maximum and minimum zoom scales of your scroll views. If you're designing an app for another developer, indicate whether or not your scroll views can zoom and by what scale. Also be aware of the default content-Size (no scaling) of your image.

CHAPTER 13

Creating Custom iOS Gestures

In general, it's best to avoid defining new gestures. Wait, what? You're probably asking yourself, Why dedicate an entire chapter to creating custom gestures only to start off by saying it should be avoided?

It's true that, for the majority of apps, Apple recommends that you not go overboard by defining *new* gestures, especially new gestures for already established behaviors. By new gestures I mean things like using a check-mark gesture for confirmation, or drawing a big X across the screen for delete. Apps are supposed to be simple; forcing a user to learn new and unnecessary gestures only increases your app's learning curve and quickly decreases its intuitive nature.

There is a place for custom gestures, however. We've talked extensively in this book about creating custom UIViews and custom animations. Because we built these views from scratch, they obviously do not support any Apple-provided gestures through UIKit, at least not out of the box. That's where this chapter comes in handy. In iOS 3.2, Apple added a built-in gesture recognizer that connects easily to any UIView through your controller. Remember the separation with Model-View-Controller. These gesture recognizers allow you to create custom views, and then hook them up seamlessly to your controllers. This means you don't have to reinvent the wheel by decrypting an array of touch patterns to add common gestures such as panning, tapping, rotating, and more.

What if we want to design a card game that allows the user to flip cards on the table or drag and rotate cards around to reposition them? Or what if we want to let the user shuffle the cards by shaking the phone? We could create a UIViewController for the board, and we know how to create a custom UIView for the card. But once the cardView is added as a subview to our boardViewController, how do we know if the user will double tap, rotate, or drag the cards? How do we know when the user will shake the phone?

In this chapter, we'll complete our journey through iOS user interface, animations, and gestures by learning how to create and manage touch- and motion-based gestures.

Detecting Touches in a UIView

There are a couple of different ways to track touches in a UIView. Touches are stored in an object called UITouch, which tracks the location, tap count, and timestamp of each touch event. The first technique we'll discuss involves overriding a series of methods in your UIView to track discrete interaction. Basically, we're creating something like this:

Tracking Touches
in a UIView

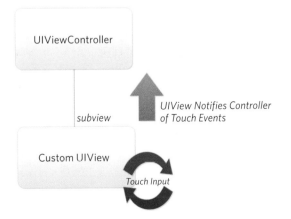

UIViewController

subview

*UIView Notifies Controller
of Touch Events*

Custom UIView

Touch Input

This technique involves adding a custom UIView as a subview to a view controller's associated view. We've done that before in Chapter 8, Creating Custom UIViews and UIViewControllers. Next, we override additional methods to our UIView (similar to the way we overrode drawRect to create a custom view) to detect touch events on the view. When our view sees a new touch event, it notifies the controller where appropriate action can be taken.

Before we can start detecting touch events in our UIViews, however, we must first check the following properties:

- userInteractionEnabled
- multipleTouchEnabled

By default, userInteractionEnabled is set to YES, allowing touch events to register, and multipleTouchEnabled is set to NO, which causes touch events to see only one touch at a time.

After deciding what types of touches we want to track by setting the userInteractionEnabled and multipleTouchEnabled Boolean operators accordingly, we need to override the following methods in the UIView:

- touchesBegan:withEvent:
- touchesMoved:withEvent:
- touchesEnded:withEvent:
- touchesCancelled:withEvent:

Each of these methods provides two parameters: an NSSet (a distinct collection of objects) of the actual UITouch events, and UIEvent, an event object that provides all of the touches in that sequence of touches (for example, if you drag an object, the UIEvent gives you access to all of the touches in the dragging motion).

Touches Began

Touches began is triggered when a UIView is first touched. By overriding this method you can either notify the controller of the touch event, or set a local variable and call setNeedsDisplay to refresh the view. The following code block demonstrates how to recognize a touchesBegan event and change the background color of the local view:

```
1    //Called when our UIView is first created
2    - (id)initWithFrame:(CGRect)frame {
3        if (self = [super initWithFrame:frame]) {
4            bgColor = [UIColor redColor];
5        }
6        return self;
7    }
8
9     //Called when our view needs display refreshed
10   - (void)drawRect:(CGRect)rect{
11       CGContextRef context = UIGraphicsGetCurrentContext();
12       [bgColor set];
13       CGContextFillRect(context, rect);
14   }
15
16   //Called when the view sees a touch event
17   - (void)touchesBegan:(NSSet *)touches withEvent:(UIEvent *)event{
18       if([bgColor isEqual:[UIColor redColor]])
19           bgColor = [UIColor blueColor];
20       else
21           bgColor = [UIColor redColor];
22       //Call set needs display to refresh our view with new color
23       [self setNeedsDisplay];
24   }
```

Lines 2 through 6 overrides the initialization of the UIView and sets a local variable called bgColor. In lines 10 through 13, bgColor is then used during the drawRect function to fill the view with a solid color. This should all look familiar from Chapter 8, Creating Custom UIViews and UIViewControllers, but basically we're setting the stage for the UIView to fill the background with a solid color that is defined as a local variable.

We detect the touch event in lines 17 through 24. Because the property userInteractionEnabled is set to YES in the UIView, if we implement the touchesBegan:withEvent method, iOS will automatically call this function whenever a touch event begins. Lines 18 through 21 are simply an if-else conditional block that toggles the bgColor variable between red and blue (if bgColor was red last touch, it will turn it blue, and vice versa). After changing the bgColor variable, we call setNeedsDisplay in line 23, which refreshes the view and changes the color.

Touches Moved

The *touches moved* method is called whenever a touch event is moved across a UIView. There is a catch, however: touchesMoved:withEvent: will be called only if the touchesBegan:withEvent: method originated in the same view. So, if someone touches a different view and then moves across another, the second view will not register a new touch moved.

Let's assume the same code block beginning with line 16 above, and append the following lines of code to implement touchesMoved:

```
1   //Called when the view sees a touch event
2   - (void)touchesMoved:(NSSet *)touches withEvent:(UIEvent *)event{
3       bgColor = [UIColor greenColor];
4       //Call set needs display to refresh our view with new color
5       [self setNeedsDisplay];
6   }
```

Just as we changed the bgColor variable on touchesBegan, here we'll change the color variable to green while the view is tracking a touchesMoved sequence.

Note

The touches moved method is called every time a touch position value is changed inside the view. This means it will be called very frequently, whenever the user drags a finger across the view, so be mindful of doing complex or resource-intense operations in this method.

Touches Ended

The *touches ended* method is called when a user's finger is raised from the display. This means that single-tap gestures call touches began first, then touches ended immediately after. A drag gesture calls touches began, followed by touches moved, and finally touches ended. This is actually how UIControl implements the button UIControlEvents such as UIControlEventTouchDown, UIControlEventTouchUpInside, UIControlEventTouchDragInside, and so on.

Let's go back to our code example. Because we know touches ended is called at the end of every touch event, we can't simply change the color to something new, otherwise both a single tap and a touches moved event will eventually call touches ended. Instead, in our touches ended method, let's change the color only if the tap count for that touch sequence was greater than two.

```
1  - (void)touchesEnded:(NSSet *)touches withEvent:(UIEvent *)event{
2      //Get a UITouch object from our touches set
3      //  so that we can count the number of taps
4      UITouch *touch = [touches anyObject];
5      if([touch tapCount] >= 2)
6          bgColor = [UIColor blackColor];
7      [self setNeedsDisplay];
8  }
```

We first must pull a UITouch object from the set of touches provided in this touch event. Because it doesn't really matter which touch object we reference (if multiple fingers touch, there will be multiple touch objects), we just get anyObject in line 4. Once we have a reference to our touch, we need only check to see if the tapCount is greater than or equal to two (line 5), and then change the color (line 6). When all is said and done, we call setNeedsDisplay in line 7 to refresh the view.

Touches Cancelled

The *touches cancelled* method is called whenever a touch sequence is interrupted by a system event, such as low memory or a phone call. You can use this method to reset the view, or store important state information for when the view is resumed. The following code block resets the background color to red when a touches cancelled event occurs:

```
1   - (void)touchesCancelled:(NSSet *)touches
                    withEvent:(UIEvent *)event{
2       bgColor = [UIColor redColor];
3       [self setNeedsDisplay];
4   }
```

Get the Code ⇒ ⇒ ⇒

Go to **fromideatoapp.com/download/example#uiview-touch** to download a project containing more examples of tracking touch events on a UIView.

Gesture Recognizers

We've learned how to track touches manually on UIViews, but there's actually a much easier way to track common gestures using gesture recognizers (UIGestureRecognizer), which were introduced in iOS 3.2. A UIGestureRecognizer is a simple class that gets associated with a UIView. When a gesture recognizer observes its configured gesture in its associated view, it automatically signals the action selector method in its target object. In other words, after we create a view, we assign it a gesture recognizer and give that recognizer an action to perform when it sees the gesture it's looking for.

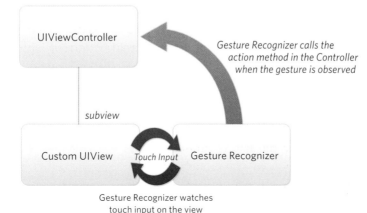

Detecting Touches with Gesture Recognizers

UIViewController

Gesture Recognizer calls the action method in the Controller when the gesture is observed

subview

Custom UIView   *Touch Input*   Gesture Recognizer

Gesture Recognizer watches touch input on the view

Apple has created six gesture recognizers, all subclasses of the UIGestureRecognizer parent class. You can use one of these predefined gesture recognizers, which will meet most of your needs out of the box, or capture the stream of touch data and create your own. For now, let's just use one of these predefined recognizers:

- UITapGestureRecognizer
- UIPinchGestureRecognizer
- UIRotationGestureRecognizer
- UIPanGestureRecognizer
- UISwipeGestureRecognizer
- UILongPressGestureRecognizer

There is no limit to the number of gesture recognizers you can associate with a view. If you want, you can have the same view associated with a pan gesture and a rotate gesture, giving you control over both the position and rotation. Similarly, you can specify the same gesture more than once, for example, registering a two-tap gesture and a three-tap gesture using a different target action.

Tip

To allow two different gesture recognizers to register touch events at the same time, you must give them permission by implementing gestureRecognizer:(first gesture recognizer) shouldRecognizeSimultaneouslyWithGestureRecognizer:(second gesture recognizer). Pay a visit to **fromideatoapp.com/reference#simulGR** for more information on simultaneous gesture recognizers.

Each gesture recognizer cycles through a series of states that are used to determine the behavior of the UIGestureRecognizer. These states (UIGestureRecognizerState) are stored as the property state in the gesture recognizer object and can be checked at any time. The gesture recognizer states include Possible, Began, Changed, Ended, Cancelled, Failed, Recognized, and Ended. Some gestures are triggered only when the state is ended, while others are triggered as the state changes. If necessary, you can check the value of the recognizer state in your handler method for conditional operations. Visit **fromideatoapp.com/reference#recognizerstates** for more information.

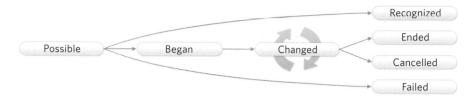

Gesture Recognizer
State Diagram

Designer Note

As we walk through the different gesture recognizer types, try
not to get lost in the code blocks or the actual implementation. Pay
close attention to the options that can be configured on each gesture
and think of how you can use them in your apps. Gesture recognizers make it easy to incorporate one-, two-, or even three-finger
swipes, pans, or taps, and again, there is no limit to the number of
gestures you can assign to a view.

UITapGestureRecognizer

The tap gesture recognizer is triggered when a stated number of taps is
recognized on the associated view using a stated number of fingers. For
example, the following code block sets up a UITapGestureRecognizer
for a single tap gesture:

```
1  UITapGestureRecognizer *oneTap = [[UITapGestureRecognizer alloc]
                                          initWithTarget:self
                                          action:@selector(handleOneTap:)];
2  oneTap.numberOfTapsRequired = 1;
3  oneTap.numberOfTouchesRequired = 1;
4  [myView addGestureRecognizer:oneTap];
5  [oneTap release];
```

In line 1, we allocate the tap gesture recognizer and set the current
controller as the target (self), with an action handleOneTap:. In lines
2 and 3, we configure the number of taps and the number of touches
required to trigger the action. In lines 4 and 5, we add the gesture
recognizer to the view and clean up memory.

In this case, when the user taps on myView once, using one finger, the gesture recognizer calls the following function in the controller:

```
1  - (void)handleOneTap:(UITapGestureRecognizer*)sender{
2      //Handle One Tap Gesture
3  }
```

Get the Code ➭ ➭ ➭

Go to **fromideatoapp.com/download/example#gesture-everything** to download a project containing more examples of the UITapGestureRecognizer.

UIPinchGestureRecognizer

The pinch gesture is triggered when a UIView receives a valid pinch open or pinch close gesture involving two touches. Unlike the tap gesture recognizer, which triggers an action when the gesture ends, the pinch gesture recognizer calls the action selector throughout the UIGestureRecognizerStateChanged state.

Because there are fewer options with the pinch gesture recognizer, the implementation is much easier:

```
1  - (void)createPinchGesture{
2      UIPinchGestureRecognizer *pinch =
          [[UIPinchGestureRecognizer alloc]
              initWithTarget:self
                  action:@selector(handlePinch:)];
3      [myView addGestureRecognizer:pinch];
4      [pinch release];
5  }
6
7  - (void)handlePinch:(UIPinchGestureRecognizer*)sender{
8      //Handle Pinch Gesture
9  }
```

This time, for convenience, the gesture creation is wrapped inside a function, createPinchGesture{}. This has no real impact on how the gesture is created; it just gives us the opportunity to look at everything in one condensed code block.

Again, you will recognize that lines 2 through 4 set up the pinch gesture. This time, there are no tap or touch options to configure—a pinch is defined as two fingers only. Lines 7 through 9 indicate where we would implement the pinch gesture handler. This function is called while a pinch gesture is detected on myView.

Get the Code ⇒ ⇒ ⇒

Go to **fromideatoapp.com/download/example#gesture-everything** to download a project containing more examples of the UIPinchGestureRecognizer.

UIRotationGestureRecognizer

The rotation gesture recognizer triggers the action selector when a two-finger rotation gesture is performed on the associated view. Just like the pinch gesture, the rotation gesture continues to call the action selector throughout the UIGestureRecognizerStateChanged state.

Again, there are fewer options with this gesture because the gesture recognizer keeps track of only the rotation angle and velocity of the change between different rotations (how fast the view is being rotated).

```
1  - (void)createRotateGesture{
2      UIRotationGestureRecognizer *r =
           [[UIRotationGestureRecognizer alloc]
               initWithTarget:self
                     action:@selector(handleRotate:)];
3      [myView addGestureRecognizer:r];
4      [r release];
5  }
6
```

```
7    - (void)handleRotate:(UIRotationGestureRecognizer*)sender{
8        //Handle Rotate Gesture
9        sender.view.transform =
             CGAffineTransformMakeRotation(sender.rotation);
10   }
```

Lines 1 through 5 perform the same function as they did in the tap and pinch recognizers. Basically, we're setting up a new recognizer, and because there are no additional options, after creating the variable in memory, we simply associate it with the view.

This time, to make things a little more interesting, I implemented an extra line of code in the action selector. Take a look at line 9. The `sender` variable provided in the call back is actually a reference to the recognizer. Because we're using a rotation gesture, I created a rotation transformation using the rotation angle in the gesture, and then applied that transformation to the view associated with the gesture. With this one line of code, the view rotates and tracks as we perform the gesture (since this method is called continuously throughout the gesture).

Transforming a
View Using Rotate
Gesture

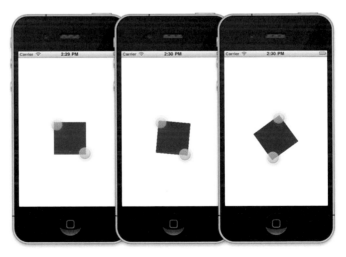

Get the Code ⇒ ⇒ ⇒

Go to **fromideatoapp.com/download/example#gesture-everything** to download a project containing more examples of the UIRotationGestureRecognizer.

UIPanGestureRecognizer

The pan (or drag) gesture is triggered when the associated UIView receives a valid drag involving a number of touches within the defined minimum and maximum. The pan gesture recognizer triggers the action selector continuously throughout the UIGestureRecognizerStateChanged state.

```
1   - (void)createPanGesture{
2       UIPanGestureRecognizer *pan =
            [[UIPanGestureRecognizer alloc]
                initWithTarget:self
                    action:@selector(handlePan:)];
3       pan.maximumNumberOfTouches = 3;
4       pan.minimumNumberOfTouches = 2;
5       [myView addGestureRecognizer:pan];
6       [pan release];
7   }
8
9   - (void)handlePan:(UIPanGestureRecognizer*)sender{
10      //Handle Panning Gesture
11  }
```

By now lines 1 and 2 should look familiar. The real difference between this code block and the code for the previous gesture recognizers is the ability to define a range of touches. In line 3 we set the maximum number of touches to three, and in line 4 we set the minimum number of touches to two. This means that if the associated UIView experiences a pan gesture using either two *or* three fingers, the gesture recognizer triggers our action selector.

Get the Code ⇒ ⇒ ⇒

Go to **fromideatoapp.com/download/example#gesture-everything** to download a project containing more examples of the UIPanGestureRecognizer.

UISwipeGestureRecognizer

The swipe gesture recognizer detects swiping actions in one or more directions on the associated view. Swipes can be detected only along the x- or y-axis: up, down, left, or right. When a swipe gesture recognizer is created, you have the option to specify the number of fingers required, and the available directions to trigger the action selector.

```
1   - (void)createSwipeGesture{
2       UISwipeGestureRecognizer *swipe =
            [[UISwipeGestureRecognizer alloc]
                initWithTarget:self
                    action:@selector(handleSwipe:)];
3       swipe.direction =
            UISwipeGestureRecognizerDirectionRight |
            UISwipeGestureRecognizerDirectionLeft;
4       [myView addGestureRecognizer:swipe];
5       [swipe release];
6   }
7
8   - (void)handleSwipe:(UIPanGestureRecognizer*)sender{
9       //Handle Swipe Gesture
10  }
```

Notice in line 3, when we set up the valid directions for the swipe, we define both the left and right directions using the pipe character | to separate the values. Also, because we did not define the number of touches required for this swipe, it defaults to one. In this example, when a user swipes the view, myView, either left or right with one finger, the swipe gesture recognizer triggers the action selector.

Get the Code ➠ ➠ ➠

Go to **fromideatoapp.com/download/example#gesture-everything** to download a project containing more examples of the UISwipeGestureRecognizer.

UILongPressGestureRecognizer

The long press gesture recognizer detects press-and-hold gestures on its associated UIView. There are four configurable options to the long press gesture recognizer: minimumPressDuration, numberOfTouches-Required, numberOfTapsRequired, and allowableMovement. The first two properties, minimumPressDuration and numberOfTouches-Required, are self-explanatory, but the purpose of the other two might not be obvious.

The numberOfTapsRequired indicates how many taps are required *before* registering the press-and-hold gesture. The default value of taps required is one, meaning that if the first tap is held, it registers as a long press gesture. However, if we change the number of taps required to two, the first tap—even if held for the minimum duration—will not register as a long press gesture.

The fourth property, allowableMovement, indicates the number of pixels the tap is allowed to move before registering the gesture as a failure. The default value for allowableMovement is 10 pixels.

```
1  - (void)createLongPressGesture{
2      UILongPressGestureRecognizer *lp =
           [[UILongPressGestureRecognizer alloc]
               initWithTarget:self
                   action:@selector(handleLP:)];
3      lp.numberOfTapsRequired = 3; //begin count on 3rd tap
4      lp.minimumPressDuration = 2;
5      lp.numberOfTouchesRequired = 1;
6      [myView addGestureRecognizer:lp];
7      [lp release];
8  }
9
10 - (void)handleLP:(UILongPressGestureRecognizer*)sender{
11     //Handle Long Press Gesture
12 }
```

In lines 3 through 5, we configure the long press gesture recognizer. Line 3 indicates that the number of taps required to begin the duration countdown is three. This means that unless the user first completes a three-tap gesture, the countdown for the long press gesture will never start. Line 4 identifies the long press duration in seconds, and line 5 identifies the number of fingers needed to complete this gesture.

Get the Code ⫶⫶ ⫶⫶ ⫶⫶

Go to **fromideatoapp.com/download/example#gesture-everything** to download a project containing more examples of the UILongPressGestureRecognizer.

Why Use UIGestureRecognizer over touchesBegan?

With two methods for tracking touches and gestures, you might ask, Why use one over the other? The answer is simple, and it comes back to our main discussion of creating and designing apps that have reusable parts.

When you create a custom UIView and track touches within the view itself, you limit your ability to reuse that view somewhere else in the app because it will have all of the associated touch methods implemented, which may not apply in every situation. Remember, in an ideal world, views are just views, and all aspects of their control is contained in the controller (Model-View-Controller).

If you create a custom UIView, however, and instead attach the necessary UIGestureRecognizer to that view from the controller, you can reuse that view in other parts of your program without the hassle of redesigning the gesture control. One use of the view can react to a swipe and another use can respond to a drag or double tap.

Designer Note

This section was very code heavy, and the concepts we've discussed most decidedly affect developers more than designers. What you should take away from this section, however, is that you can effectively design UI controls that are easy to implement and easy to reuse. When designing your UI, know that your developer might be able to use a UIGestureRecognizer rather than touches methods in your view. Try to visualize your UI as components that a developer can use and reuse, and incorporate gestures that can easily be implemented using UIGestureRecognizer.

Developer Note

Besides the Apple-defined gestures used in this section, Apple allows you to implement your own UIGestureRecognizer subclass, giving you the ability to track the touches stream manually and create gestures for things like a check mark, circle, and so on. To implement a custom gesture, after creating a UIGestureRecognizer subclass, you *must* call `#import <UIKit/UIGestureRecognizer Subclass.h>` in your header file. This allows your subclass to override the `touchesBegan`, `touchesEnded`, `touchesMoved`, and `touchesCancelled` methods of the UIGestureRecognizer. Visit **fromideatoapp.com/reference#gesturesubclass** for more information and a complete tutorial on how to create a custom gesture recognizer.

Motion Gestures

The final topic we'll discuss here is the motion of an iOS device. Just as touch gestures act as inputs to your apps, an iOS device can use data from its internal accelerometer and three-axis gyroscope to detect physical motion and the orientation of the device. So while touch inputs are commonly seen as the primary input for an app, you can also accept input from the device itself.

Note

The methods described in this section are defined in the UIResponder class, which is the parent class to UIView, UIViewController, and all of the other UIKit classes we've discussed. However, as of iOS 4.2, only the immediate subclasses of UIResponder forward events up the responder chain (UIView and UIViewController). While code compiles without errors if we override these methods in other subclasses of UIResponder, only the UIView and UIViewController actually respond.

There are two ways to use motion input on your device. You can catch an Apple-defined shake gesture, where iOS monitors input automatically and signals when a valid shake gesture has started, or you can capture a live stream of raw data from the device's accelerometer or gyroscope.

Shake Gestures in iOS

A shake gesture is triggered when an iOS device is moved abruptly, followed by little or no movement. A shake gesture is not a continuous event. If your device shakes constantly, or moves around, iOS may signal the start of a shake gesture, but cancel it after deciding the gesture is no longer valid and is likely the event of random movement. To capture a shake gesture in a UIViewController, you must set up the view controller as the first responder. A responder in iOS apps is an object that can receive and handle events from the system. By setting up the view controller as the first responder, we're telling iOS to send any motion gesture information to the view controller first. To set the view controller up as a first responder, you must add the following lines of code to the .m file:

```
1  -(void)viewDidAppear:(BOOL)animated{
2      [super viewDidAppear:animated];
3      [self becomeFirstResponder];
4  }
5
6  -(BOOL)canBecomeFirstResponder{
7      return YES;
8  }
```

The first bit of code we need to add is in the `viewDidAppear` method of the view controller (lines 1 through 4). Recalling our discussion about the view life cycle in Chapter 5, User Interface Controllers and Navigation, the `viewDidAppear` method is called immediately after the view controller's associated view is displayed on the screen. At this point (line 3), we'll call the method, `becomeFirstResponder`, which signals iOS that we want the view controller to receive all system messages first. Finally, we need to add a method that signals we are allowed to become first responder. When iOS sees a call for an object to become first responder, it will first call `canBecomeFirstResponder` in that object to see if the operation is permitted. In lines 6 through 8, we implement this method and simply return YES.

> **Developer Note**
>
> Instead of always returning YES, you can take advantage of the `canBecomeFirstResponder` method by adding a conditional return. For example, if the app has a preference to enable or disable shake gestures, instead of returning YES here, you can simply return the value of that preference. This enables or disables the view controller ability to become first responder thus enabling or disabling the shake gesture.

Recognizing Shake Motion Events

Motion events respond to a method pattern just as touch events respond to the `touchesBegan`, `touchesEnded`, and `touchesCancelled` methods. When motion is detected by iOS, a UIEvent is created with the type UIEventTypeMotion and the subtype UIEventSubtypeMotionShake, and then passed on to our motion response methods. As of iOS 4.2, *iOS recognizes only the shake gesture motion type.*

While touch events include multiple touches and a tap count, motion events include only a valid shake gesture or *not* a valid shake gesture. The following methods can be implemented in the view controller to catch motion events. Remember, unless your view controller is set up as the first responder, these methods will be ignored:

- `motionBegan:withEvent:`
- `motionEnded:withEvent:`
- `motionCancelled:withEvent:`

Designer Note

You can use shake motion gestures as components of your UI. Apple has created a set of APIs that allow you to easily incorporate gestures such as shake-to-undo and shake-to-redo in your app. If you create workflows that allow the user to edit and manage data, consider building in a shake gesture as a part of the workflow.

The following code block creates and adds a UILabel named "status" in the view controller's `viewDidLoad` method, and then adds motion response methods.

```
1   - (void)viewDidLoad {
2       [super viewDidLoad];
3       CGRect lframe = CGRectMake(0, 0, 320, 30);
4       status = [[UILabel alloc] initWithFrame:lframe];
5       status.text = @"No Shake Detected";
6       status.textAlignment = UITextAlignmentCenter;
7
8       [self.view addSubview:status];
9       [status release];
10  }
11  - (void)motionBegan:(UIEventSubtype)motion
              withEvent:(UIEvent *)event{
12      status.text = @"Shake Motion Started";
13  }
14
15  - (void)motionCancelled:(UIEventSubtype)motion
                  withEvent:(UIEvent *)event{
16      status.text = @"Shake Motion Cancelled";
17  }
18
```

```
19  - (void)motionEnded:(UIEventSubtype)motion
            withEvent:(UIEvent *)event{
20      status.text = @"Shake Motion Ended";
21  }
```

In lines 1 through 10, we set up the UILabel, status, which is a local variable, and then add it as a subview to the view controller's associated view (line 8). Lines 11 through 21 implement the motion response methods. In line 11, we catch the start of a shake gesture by implementing motionBegan:withEvent. To help identify this, we change the text in our status label to "Shake Motion Started". In line 15, we catch whether the gesture was cancelled by iOS, and update the label accordingly. Remember that a shake gesture is cancelled if iOS decides that the shake is no longer valid (for example, wild shaking of the device is not indicative of a deliberate gesture). Finally, in line 19, we implement the motionEnded:withEvent method. At this point, we can consider the shake gesture as valid. If you implant a custom shake-to-do-something awesome-feature, use the motionEnded method to ensure that the gesture was not accidental (and cancelled by iOS).

Get the Code ➡ ➡ ➡

Go to **fromideatoapp.com/download/example#shake-gestures** to download a project containing more examples of Shake Gestures.

Bonus Material Online

I ran out of space! My editor tells me I need to cut pages from the book—and I have so much more to tell you. So I took the last twelve pages of this chapter and created online bonus material where we continue our discussion on how to implement custom motion gestures using raw data from the accelerometer and gyroscope at **fromideatoapp.com/bonus-material**.

Custom Gestures

We just learned how to use gestures to add unique functions to your iOS apps. Unlike most desktop applications, iOS apps are not limited to input driven by buttons or controls. Physical motion of the device itself or multi-touch gestures on the device screen can provide a truly immersive experience for users.

Get the Code ⇒⇒⇒

You can build this app as we go, or go to **fromideatoapp.com/ downloads/blueprints** to download the completed project file FI2ADemo and follow along.

Overview

Our goal for this blueprint is simple. We want to let the user drag the countdown controller (added in the previous blueprint) across the screen using two fingers. We've talked about two methods for tracking a user's finger on the screen:

- Implementing touchesBegan, touchesMoved, and touchesCancelled in HUDView (a UIView subclass)
- Adding a UIPanGestureRecognizer to the countdown timer from the T2_TableViewController class

Now we need to consider how and why to implement one method or the other. As you know, we downloaded the CountdownViewController and HUDView classes in the previous blueprint. Having not written the code yourself, it might not be the best idea to start overriding methods to add the dragging behavior. We're also adding the countdown view to the navigation controller of the T2_TableViewController. The last thing we want to do is isolate controller methods inside a view, especially when we're already adding the view to another controller's associated view and now our own (self.navigationController.view).

In light of this, it makes sense to add this function to the Countdown-ViewController by creating a UIPanGestureRecognizer and associating it to the view at the time of creation. This way the CountdownView-Controller remains untouched, giving us the ability to reuse this class in the future when we might not want the user to move it around and our controller class maintains control over the UI's behaviors.

To give the user the ability to drag the countdown timer around the screen using a UIPanGestureRecognizer, we'll perform the following steps:

1. Create a CGPoint reference in the T2_TableViewController header file to store the initial value of the touch event and define a method for handling the actual panning gesture.

2. Create a UIPanGestureRecognizer and associate it with the CountdownViewController's view before presenting it on the screen.

3. Reposition the CountdownViewController's view based on the relative motion of the panning gesture.

Step 1

First we need to add two things to the T2_TableViewController header file: a CGPoint to track where the panning motion starts, and a handler method to take care of the actual panning action. By now, you should be comfortable creating new instance variables and defining new methods, so let's add the following code block:

```
1  #import <UIKit/UIKit.h>
2  #import "CountdownViewController.h"
3  @interface T2_TableViewController : UITableViewController
       <CountdownViewControllerDelegate> {
4  CGPoint firstPoint;
5  }
6
7  - (void)panCountdownHUD:(UIPanGestureRecognizer*)panGesture;
8  @end
```

In line 4, we add a variable named firstPoint to the class interface, and in line 7 we declare the panning gesture method. Notice that in line 7, the panning action method receives as a parameter the panning gesture itself. We'll use this to maintain reference to the countdown view as it is moved.

Step 2

The next step is to actually create the panning gesture. Because we're making the countdown view controller in the didSelectRowAtIndexPath method of T2_TableViewController, it makes sense to create our gesture here as well. We simply allocate a new variable, define the number of touches required, and then associate it with the CountdownController-View's view.

We'll add the following code block to the didSelectRowAtIndexPath method immediately following the creation of count, our local variable of CountdownViewController:

```
1   // Create a new UIPanGestureRecognizer
2   //    Set the target of the gesture action to self
3   //    Set the action method to panCountdownHUD:
4   UIPanGestureRecognizer *pan = [[UIPanGestureRecognizer alloc]
        initWithTarget:self
        action:@selector(panCountdownHUD:)];
5
6   // Define the number of touches required
7   pan.minimumNumberOfTouches = 2;
8
9   // Add the panning gesture recognizer to the
10  //    view of our countdown clock and then
11  //    release our panning gesture (memory management)
12   [count.view addGestureRecognizer:pan];
13   [pan release];
```

In line 4, we create the new UIPanGestureRecognizer, assigning the target as self (T2_TableViewContoller) and the action as panCount downHUD:. Next, in line 7 we define the number of touches required, followed by line 12 where we associate the gesture recognizer with the countdown view controller's view. In line 13, we maintain proper memory management by releasing the pan gesture.

Step 3

The last step is to implement the panCountdownHUD method so that as the user drags the view with two fingers, the position of the countdown view controller's view tracks to follow. We do this by storing the location of the view when the gesture first begins, then calculating the difference between where the gesture is now and where it started. Finally, we apply a new center to the view based on these calculations.

```
1   - (void)panCountdownHUD:(UIPanGestureRecognizer*)panGesture{

2

3   // Check the gesture recognizer state.  If things have just begun, save

4   //   the current location of the countdown view controller's view

5   if([panGesture state] == UIGestureRecognizerStateBegan)

6         firstPoint = panGesture.view.center;

7

8   // Calculate the difference (x,y) based on the current

9   //   position of the panning motion

10  CGPoint diff = [panGesture

              translationInView:self.navigationController.view];

11

12  // Calculate a new center based on our original center

13  //   and the difference created by our panning motion

14  CGPoint newCenter = CGPointMake(firstPoint.x + diff.x,
                                  firstPoint.y + diff.y);

15

16  // Apply the new center to our countdown view controller's view

17  panGesture.view.center = newCenter;

18  }
```

And that's it! If you build and run the project, you should be able to reposition the countdown view controller by dragging it with two fingers. If you are using the iOS Simulator, go back and change the touches required from two to one. This will trigger the panning gesture when only one finger is used. Because the iOS Simulator can't simulate multiple touches during a panning gesture, you'll only see the two-finger panning gesture on an actual iOS device.

You can see the added advantage of using gestures to improve usability and add functions. Remember, we also learned how to implement the pinch-zoom gesture. If you want to take this project further by adding a pinch-to-scale up or down gesture, you could do so using UIPinch-GestureRecognizer. You could also implement a swipe-to-cancel feature using the UISwipeGestureRecognizer. Feel free to download the project files and build on them.

Get the Code ⇒ ⇒ ⇒

Download FI2ADemo at **fromideatoapp.com/downloads/blueprints** to see samples from this blueprint and more.

Note from the Author

Thank you for reading *From Idea to App: Creating iOS UI, Animations and Gestures*! I truly hope you enjoyed the book and learned something along the way. Be sure to check out the resources that are available at **fromideatoapp.com** and do not hesitate to contact me with questions and/or comments either from the book's website (**fromideatoapp.com**) or directly @shawnwelch (**twitter.com/shawnwelch**). If after reading the book you decide to make an app, let me know! I'd love to see what you guys create, I might even be your first customer. :)

Keep it simple, keep it effective, make it memorable.

—Shawn

Index

WATCH
READ
CREATE

Meet Creative Edge.

A new resource of unlimited books, videos and tutorials for creatives from the world's leading experts.

Creative Edge is your one stop for inspiration, answers to technical questions and ways to stay at the top of your game so you can focus on what you do best—being creative.

All for only $24.99 per month for access—any day any time you need it.

creative
edge

peachpit.com/creativeedge